HOLY DAYS:
HOLIDAYS

HOLY DAYS:
HOLIDAYS

*by Judith Ritchie
and Vicki Niggemeyer*

illustrated by Toni Pepera

mott media
BOX 236, MILFORD, MI. 48042

For Bill, Jeff, Jennifer, John, Lynn, and Paul

Scripture references are taken from *The Living Bible, Paraphrased* (Tyndale House, 1971) unless otherwise specified.

Library of Congress Cataloging in Publication Data

Ritchie, Judith
  Holy days.

  Bibliography: p.
  SUMMARY: Discusses 16 familiar holidays including Easter, Labor Day, and birthdays. Suggested activities and Bible verses for each of these days are included.
  1. Holidays—Juvenile literature. 2. Fasts and feasts—Juvenile literature. [1. Holidays. 2. Fasts and feasts. 3. Christian life] I. Niggemeyer, Vicki, 1944- joint author. II. Pepera, Toni. III. Title.
  GT3933.R57   394.2'6   78-23841
  ISBN 0-915134-48-9

CONTENTS

PREFACE

The word *holiday* comes from the Anglo-Saxon *haligdaeg* which means holy day. Years ago, the only days set apart for celebrations were those honoring sacred events. Today holidays for many people are merely vacations from school or work.

Because of this, we feel that children are being denied a background they are entitled to. Therefore, we wrote *Holy Days: Holidays* to explain familiar American holidays from a Christian point of view. Although written on a child's level, our book is also a resource guide for parents and teachers. At the end of each chapter are Bible verses from *The Living Bible, Paraphrased* which can be memorized, as well as a section with activities to make each holiday holy once again.

We hope parents will read this book along with their children as each holiday approaches. Children and teachers can share the ideas to add another dimension to their study of holidays. Classroom activities can be used in the Christian school or Sunday School. Many projects are suitable for public schools.

We are grateful to the many people who encouraged and supported the writing of this book. Special thanks go to our husbands, Chuck and Joe, as well as Chaplain Thomas Condon, Aase McTamney, Emily Kast, Neva J. Korn, and Florence Pauls.

It is our prayer that this book will help Christians everywhere spread the word that holidays *are* holy days.

Judith Ritchie
Vicki Niggemeyer

1

NEW YEAR'S DAY

On January 1 we celebrate a new beginning. Bells ring, confetti flies, people shout. New Year's Day is crowded with parades, football games, parties. But it is also a time to ask God's help in the year ahead.

Would you like to celebrate New Year's Day two or three times a year? Long ago, maybe all the way back to Adam and Eve, people rejoiced at the end of each growing season. To them, each harvest was a new beginning.

Julius Caesar decreed the Romans to change the many small celebrations to one big festival on January 1. This day honored their god of beginning, Janus. He had two faces, one looking back and one ahead.

Some of Rome's ancient new year customs are still part of our celebration. People then believed they should confess their sins at the beginning of each year. They also believed in driving off evil spirits with shouts, drums, and noise. Today we know that God protects us from the evil spirits. But we still like to make much noise for happiness with horns, bells, and sirens.

The Chinese also celebrate their New Year with noise. Loud gongs, crashing cymbals, beating drums, and exploding firecrackers are heard for miles. (The firecrackers are always red, the Chinese color for good omens.) Adding to the noise are babbling crowds of people parading through the streets.

Because the Chinese follow an ancient calendar, their New Year falls sometime between January 21 and February 19.

While most of the world welcomes the New Year loudly, some people greet it quietly. The Jewish New Year, Rosh Hashanah, has always been a time of soul searching and repentance. Like the Chinese, the Jewish people follow their own ancient calendar. Therefore, their New Year falls between September and October. A highlight of their ritual is the blowing of the shofar. This is a beautifully carved horn which is formed from a ram's horn. When the horn is blown, it reminds the Jewish people of their beginnings. But above all, it reminds them that they are God's people. By asking God to forgive their sins of the past year, they can look forward with hope to the new year.

Like the Jewish people, Christians began to feel the need to include God in their New Year celebrations. So in 1770 members of St. George's Methodist Church in Philadelphia held the first watch-night service. Just before midnight on New Year's Eve, they gathered to ask God's help in the coming year.

Services like this continue to take place today. Some are like regular church services with singing, praying and communion. Others are held in homes where Christians greet the new year informally with singing and fellowship. But above all, it is a time to think about God's place in the new year.

Some people write down ways they want to change in order to have a better new year. For example, I will control my temper, or, I will visit a sick person each week. These firm decisions are called resolutions. Christians ask God to help them keep these promises to improve.

The new year will bring many changes—more friends, another birthday, and new things to learn. It may bring sadness and sometimes disappointment. But it will also bring another year to live in God's great big beautiful world. With His help we can make each year better than the one before.

> Commit everything you do to the Lord. Trust him to help you do it and he will.
>
> Psalm 37:5

NEW YEAR'S DAY ACTIVITIES

Go With God Sign

1. *white paper plates*
2. *red and green paint*
3. *black marker*
4. *yellow and dark construction paper*
5. *popsicle sticks*

Glue together two paper plates (back to back) with a popsicle stick between them. Paint one side green, the other side red. Let dry. Cut from the dark construction paper a two-faced Janus head. Glue to the red side of plate. From the yellow construction paper cut a triangle and glue to the green side. Above the Janus head write STOP with black marker. Above the triangle write GO.

Hold the signs and discuss the meaning of the following symbols:

circle = eternal
darkness = sin (Ephesians 5:11)
yellow triangle = trinity
red plate = stop sinning
green plate = go with God

Also discuss:

Where did the name January come from? What does it mean?

Janus represents one of the old gods. What or who are some other gods people worship today? Consider television and movie actors, singers.

Read Revelation 22:13. People believed that only Janus could see backward and forward. What about God? Other gods are limited, but the one true God has no limitations.

Resolution Box

   1. *oatmeal box*
   2. *paint*
   3. *construction paper*

Paint the oatmeal box and let it dry. Cut Christian symbols from the construction paper, for example, cross, butterfly, fish, lamb, dove, star. On a strip of construction paper write the verse, "I can do all things through Christ which strengtheneth me" (Philippians 4:13, King James Version). Glue all of the above onto the painted oatmeal box.

Have friends or classmates make resolutions or do this alone. Write the resolutions on small index cards and drop them into the box. (Number of cards will depend on the age of your group.) At the end of each month reread the cards and discuss success or failure.

Read Through the Bible in One Year

Agree among your family or classmates that you will read from the Bible each day so that at the end of one year you will have made it through the entire Bible. Tracts are available at local bookstores or your church with Bible-reading schedules. If you read three chapters a day, you will finish in approximately one year. For variety you can read two chapters from the Old Testament and one chapter from the New Testament each day.

Bulletin Board—"GOD HELPS US TURN OVER A NEW LEAF"

    1. green and white construction paper
    2. markers or crayons

Have your entire class make a list of bad habits. Ask your teacher to divide the class in half. One group draws pictures on the white construction paper of bad habits (for example, children fighting). The other group draws pictures of opposite behavior (children cooperating). Teacher or students make green construction paper leaves. Staple a picture to each leaf and place on the bulletin board.

Use Psalm 37:5 to emphasize *how* God helps us.

Classroom Activity

Have students write individual letters to God. Each person can tell God about something that he or she did last year for which he/she is sincerely sorry. (This is confession of sin.) Next the writer folds the letter several times to ensure privacy of the content.

Now the teacher collects the letters into a large bag. She staples the top securely. Then she prays aloud asking God to forgive the sins contained in the paper bag. Take the bag outside and, if possible, burn it. If this is not possible, put the bag into a trash container that is secure from prying eyes of children who might want to get into the bag. Back in the classroom, let the children look up verses that tell how God forgives, for example, 1 John 1:9.

(Contributed by Florence W. Pauls)

New Year's Wish

Wish everyone you see a blessed New Year by saying, "God bless you in the New Year!" Be sure to keep a smile on your face. Can you explain how Christians can be happy all the new year?

2
VALENTINE'S DAY

The holiday of love, Valentine's Day, is celebrated on February 14. We buy cards at the store or make them out of red paper, paste, and lace. Some people give candy and flowers. But God gave us the greatest valentine—Jesus.

The beautiful red and white valentine box at school is stuffed to the brim with cards. "Are you ready?" asks the teacher. "Yes!" shout the children. They eagerly watch as she passes the valentines around. How did these little cards become so important and exciting to us?

Thousands of years ago, the Romans had a holiday called Lupercalia. They believed that one of their gods, Lupercus, protected them from the many wild, hungry wolves that roamed their land. To thank him for his help, the people had a big celebration each year in the middle of February. It was a day of eating, dancing, and games. Young men picked partners for this celebration by drawing an unmarried girl's name from a bowl.

Years later, after Jesus died and came to life again, some Romans became Christians and gave up their old gods. They believed that Jesus was the true God and worshipped Him. However, many others did not believe in Jesus and tried to harm the people who did. This hatred ended only when the Roman emperor Constantine became a Christian in the early fourth century.

Then the old gods of Rome were no longer worshipped. But Lupercalia had been such a happy time that the people wanted to keep it. So instead of honoring Lupercus, they dedicated this day to a man of the church.

The man selected was Valentine. He lived so long ago we do not know much about him. But we do know that he was a priest, and some believe he was killed for his faith one February 14 in Rome. After Lupercalia was changed to Valentine's Day, it became known as a day for lovers.

Gradually, Valentine's Day spread to many countries, each adding its own customs. In Italy young girls get up before sunrise and watch from their windows. They believe their husband will be the first unmarried man who passes by.

Denmark has an unusual valentine called a joking letter. A boy sending one does not sign his name on it. Instead, he uses a code of dots—one dot for each letter of his name. If the girl guesses who the boy is and tells him, he rewards her with an Easter egg the following Easter.

Over the years the word "valentine" has come to mean different things: sweethearts, verses with pictures, and gifts of candy or flowers. But most of all, the word "valentine" has come to mean love.

Long before the Roman celebration of Lupercalia, God introduced love into the world. Remember Adam and Eve? They were the world's first sweethearts. God loved them and wanted them to love each other.

He also tells us to love one another. "Dear friends, let us practice loving each other, for love comes from God and those who are loving and kind show that they are the children of God, and that they are getting to know him better. But if a person isn't loving and kind, it shows that he doesn't know God—for God is love" (1 John 4:7–8).

Valentines are exciting, because they are little messages of love. We give them to everyone—family, teachers, friends, and neighbors. But the best one of all is from God. "The free gift of God is eternal life through Jesus Christ" (Romans 6:23). Jesus is God's valentine to the world.

> God loved the world so much
> that he gave his only Son.
> John 3:16

VALENTINE'S DAY ACTIVITIES

Make your own valentines.
1. *red construction paper*
2. *paper doilies, lace, and ribbon for trim*
3. *crayons or felt-tip pens*

   Instead of buying valentines, make one for each classmate. Cut out hearts and decorate with doilies, lace or ribbon. On each one write a favorite Bible verse or thought, such as "Jesus is God's valentine to you" or "God loves you."

Joking Valentines

1. *red construction paper*
2. *crayons or black felt-tip pens*

   Have your class cut out hearts. Students should put one black dot for each letter in their name (Jane = ...). Place all hearts in a box and shake. Let each person draw one. Each child has three guesses to find the maker of the joking heart.

Bulletin Board—"SWEETHEARTS FROM THE BIBLE"

1. *red and white construction paper*
2. *doilies and ribbon to frame bulletin board*

   Make large hearts from red construction paper. On white paper, have class members draw pictures of some Bible sweethearts (Adam and Eve, Abraham and Sarah, Ruth and Boaz, Mary and Joseph). Attach the pictures to the hearts and arrange them on the bulletin board with the ribbon and doilies.

Love Valentine
   Give a love valentine—yourself—to someone lonely. Give your time to someone by writing them a letter, visiting a shut-in, making heart-shaped cookies and giving them away.

Valentine Placemats

    1. large pieces of white construction paper
    2. red construction paper, tape

Make a placemat for everyone in your family from white paper. Make a heart from a 15.2 centimeter (6 inch) piece of red construction paper. Fold the heart in half. Glue or paste the right side of the heart onto the left side of the placemat of white construction paper. Across the top of each mat print the name of a family member. Write on the inside of the heart a special favor or job you will do for that person. Tape the heart closed. Open the heart at mealtime to find the happy message.

Bible Search
    1. Why is Jesus God's valentine to you and me? (Matthew 18:11 and 1 John 4:10)
    2. How do you give a valentine to God? (John 15:14 and Psalm 1)
    3. If you love God, will you be likely to hurt His feelings—or is it possible to hurt His feelings? (Matthew 23:37–39 and Genesis 6:6)
    4. Does God stop loving us when we do something wrong? (Jeremiah 31:3 and Romans 5:8)
                       (Contributed by Florence W. Pauls)

Talk Time

Read 1 John 4:7–8.

Tell one way you can show that you love another person—without saying a word. Write this out, giving details of exactly how you would do this. Would it be in secret, for example, or would it be all right for everyone to see? Or would it matter? Would you touch the person? Would it be necessary for the other person to know who did this? Or would it be best that it be kept a secret?

Can you love people who look ugly? Or do you find that as you get to know people, you forget how they look? Have you at some time in your life come to like (or love) a person you at first thought was ugly? Tell someone about it.

Do you want people to like you for what you are rather than the way you look? Since you don't pay for your clothes, you may not always be happy with what you wear. Do you think people would like you better if you had different clothes? If so, would they be liking you or your clothes? Talk about it. Are clothes the thing that is important? Or, do nice clothes just make you comfortable so that you can be your real self?

(Contributed by Florence W. Pauls)

3
ST. PATRICK'S DAY

On March 17 people all over the world honor St. Patrick, the patron saint of Ireland. Americans celebrate with parades in the cities, by making shamrocks at school, and by wearing something green. These things are reminders of St. Patrick, a great servant of God.

Long ago, in the fifth century, a boy named Patrick had a terrible thing happen to him. But God turned it into something special.

When Patrick was sixteen years old, pirates attacked the tiny English village where he lived. It was late at night when Patrick awoke to shouts of "Help! Help!" Terrified, he ran outside. He saw that his house was in flames. People were screaming and running in all directions.

Suddenly, some of the pirates grabbed Patrick. "Mother! Father!" he yelled. The invaders dragged the struggling Patrick to their ship and sailed away to a pagan land called Ireland. There they sold him as a slave.

For six long years Patrick worked as a slave, taking care of his master's sheep. He was very lonesome and homesick. Like many people, he knew about Jesus but did not have His Spirit in his heart. Now he needed a real friend, someone he could talk with everyday. So he asked Jesus to come into his heart and be that friend.

One night in a dream God told Patrick that a boat was waiting for him. Later he escaped and reached a seaport, and a boat was there just as God had promised.

When Patrick had been home again for a few years, God gave him another message in a dream. In this dream a man brought him a letter which said, "The voice of the Irish ... asks thee, boy, come and walk with us once more." God was calling Patrick back to Ireland to tell the people about Jesus. So once more he left home. This time he traveled to France to study God's Word.

After years of preparation, Patrick was ready to go back to Ireland. Because God cared about the Irish, Patrick cared about them too. Through this humble man, the Lord healed the sick and changed lives.

Patrick spent the rest of his life telling the Irish of God's love for them. In fifty years he built over three hundred churches and baptized thousands of people. He started schools for the children and taught Latin, the language of the church, to each baptized person.

Later, during a sad time in history called the Dark Ages, barbarians ruled the world. These cruel people tried to stamp out education. But in Ireland the spark of knowledge survived mainly because of Patrick's churches and schools.

Strange stories about Patrick were told everywhere. The stories became legends, and some of them are still with us today. One is that Patrick charmed the snakes right out of Ireland. It is said that Patrick built a drum and beat it until his arms ached, driving every last snake into the sea. When they were all gone, he blessed the land so they would never return.

Another legend tells of a flaming pile of snow. Once when Patrick and his followers were on a mountaintop, they were so cold they were in danger of freezing to death. Patrick told the men to heap up snowballs until there was a gigantic pile. When the pile was finished, he breathed on it, and the snow turned into a huge bonfire.

People also said that Patrick loved the green shamrock

because its three tiny leaves reminded him of the Holy Trinity—Father, Son, and Holy Spirit. Perhaps this is why many people love the little plant still.

One thing we know for sure is that God loved Patrick, and Patrick loved God. Out of a terrible experience, a slave and the Irish found Jesus.

> Trust the Lord completely . . . In everything you do, put God first, and he will direct you and crown your efforts with success.
>
> Proverbs 3:5–6

ST. PATRICK'S DAY ACTIVITIES

Shamrock Sponge

> 1. *sponge*
> 2. *grass seed*
> 3. *shallow saucer*

One week before St. Patrick's Day, cut a sponge in the shape of a shamrock. Moisten the sponge and roll in grass seed. Put it in a saucer and keep damp. In a few days you will have a living and growing shamrock.

Make one for a class, one for a family, or one for a friend.

Shamrocks to Wear and Share

> 1. *green construction paper*
> 2. *glue*
> 3. *copies of the following quote: "If you cannot explain so simple a mystery as the shamrock, how can you hope to understand one so profound as the Holy Trinity." St. Patrick*

Cut out shamrocks and glue a quote to each. When you wear the shamrock, share with others the story of the Trinity and why it makes us recall St. Patrick.

St. Patrick's Day Mural

> 1. *paper for mural background (roll of newsprint)*
> 2. *crayons*
> 3. *pencils*

Divide mural paper into following sections:
Patrick captured by pirates
Patrick tending master's animals
Dream of man with letter
Patrick as priest
Teaching and healing

After mural is completed, role play events pictured. Discuss Patrick's feelings in each situation.

Bulletin Board—NEWSPAPER FRONT PAGE

Through pictures and reports (depending on your age level) present bulletin board as a newspaper front page. Bold headline: PATRICK KIDNAPPED!! or FLASH! GOD SAVES EDUCATION THROUGH ST. PATRICK! Suggested column headings: Barbarians Invade Ireland, Education in Danger, Priest Refuses to Let Spark Die. End with headline: A GRATEFUL WORLD CELEBRATES—MARCH 17.

Instead of making a bulletin board from a newspaper, print headlines on a sheet of paper. Write stories about St. Patrick's exciting life.

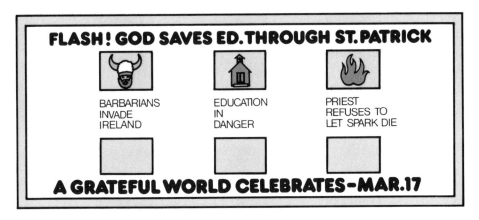

Talk Time

Can you think of an object which you could use to help describe God to someone else? What is it? Explain how the shamrock can help you describe God to someone who doesn't know Him.

St. Patrick's Day Prayer

Thank you God for missionaries like St. Patrick. Help me to be a missionary on my street, in my school, in my home. Help me trust in You as completely as Patrick did. In Jesus name I pray, Amen.

4
APRIL FOOL'S DAY

God wants everyone to be happy, and that's what this holiday is all about. We don't decorate the house or make special things for it at school. But surprises lurk everywhere just waiting to spring at any moment.

DANGER!!
This page is covered with millions of teeny-weeny black bugs. Look out! They are crawling up your arms!
APRIL FOOL!

April Fool's Day is a fun time when everyone delights in playing harmless pranks and jokes on others. This teasing holiday began because the Christian European countries refused to use the Roman calendar. Instead, their new year celebration started on March 25 and ended April 1. They had a week-long celebration filled with visiting, dinners, and giving gifts.

One of these countries (France) finally gave in and adopted the Roman calendar in the late 1500s, and January became the first month of the year. But for a time, some people kept forgetting the change. When they did, others teased them with gag gifts and called them April fools. Gradually, this led to the tricks and jokes we play on each other today.

God likes to surprise us too. He made Spring a mischievous

time of year. As bright yellow daffodils peep from the ground, He often sprinkles them with snowflakes. Or He may unexpectedly change warm spring breezes to blustering winds. These tricks don't hurt anyone—they just fool us. As long as our fun remains harmless, the words "April Fool" will bring laughter to our world.

> A happy face means a glad heart.
>
> Proverbs 15:13

APRIL FOOL'S DAY ACTIVITIES

Talk Time
Discuss the difference between harmless and harmful pranks. What April fool jokes are fun and which ones are cruel?

April Fool's Cake

1. *favorite cake mix*
2. *surprise to fold into batter*

Bake your favorite cake and fold into batter a surprise. This may be either an unmeltable object (such as a small metal cross or coin) or a fruit filling which will not be seen until the cake is cut. Discuss that many blessings are often disguised. The wise man understands this, the fool does not.

Bulletin Board—"WHICH ARE YOU—WISE OR FOOLISH?"

1. *poster board*
2. *construction paper (various colors)*
3. *markers or crayons*

Make signposts from brown construction paper and white poster board. Make road, heaven, and hell from appropriate colors of construction paper.

Read Galatians 5:18–26. On the signposts, write the qualities of foolish and wise people. Arrange the signs on the bulletin board to point to heaven or hell, whichever they are leading to.

Across the bottom of the bulletin board write the following phrases: Be wise and walk in the Spirit (idea from Galatians 5:22–25). The foolish walk away and shall *not* inherit the Kingdom of God (idea from Galatians 5:21).

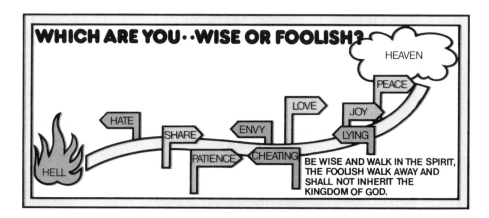

April Fool's Day Bible Quiz

There are 118 verses in the Bible that have something to say about being a fool. Look up the following passages of Scripture and find out why we are sometimes foolish.

1. A man is a FOOL who says, "_____" (Psalm 14:1).
2. Only FOOLS insist on _____ (Proverbs 20:3).
3. A FOOL shows his _____ (Proverbs 12:16).
4. A man is a FOOL to _____ himself (Proverbs 28:26).
5. A FOOL will not _____ (Ecclesiastes 4:5).
6. A FOOL _____ too much. (Proverbs 10:14).
7. A man only FOOLS himself when he thinks _____ will give him happiness (Ecclesiastes 5:10).
8. We are FOOLISH people when we do not _____ the Bible (Luke 24:25).

Answers:

8. believe	4. trust
7. money	3. temper
6. talks	2. quarreling
5. work	1. "There is no God"

(Contributed by Neva J. Korn)

5
LENT

Unlike most holiday seasons, Lent is not a time for fun and games. Instead, it is a season to remember Jesus' sacrifice and thank Him for taking away our sins.

Once a little boy heard grown-ups all around him talking about lint. He looked at his coat sleeves, no lint there. He felt in his pockets, no lint there. One morning after church, he even looked on the altar. No lint! As the boy grew up, he finally realized that the word was not "lint" but Lent, a season of the church.

Lent begins forty days before Easter and represents the forty days Jesus spent in the wilderness fasting and praying. During these forty days, we can also fast (give up food) and pray. Because Lent is so serious, many people have one last rousing celebration before it begins.

The biggest day of this celebration is Shrove Tuesday, the last day before Lent. Shrove comes from an Old English word *shrifan* which means to confess one's sins. The English call this day Pancake Tuesday. Long ago, pancakes were made to use up the milk, eggs, and fat forbidden by the Lenten fast. This custom continues today. In Germany it is called Fasnacht (Eve of the Fast). The Germans use up these same foods. But instead of pancakes, they make rectangular doughnuts called fastnachtkuchen.

In America the celebration is called Mardi gras which is French for fat Tuesday. Long ago, on Shrove Tuesday, the people of France paraded a fat ox through the streets of Paris. In 1827 students returning to America brought this custom to New Orleans where many French people lived. The day has now become a time for parades, pageants, and parties. These big noisy celebrations usually continue right up to the stroke of midnight on Shrove Tuesday. And then ... Ash Wednesday arrives, and the Lenten season begins.

The name Ash Wednesday comes from a church custom begun in the fourth century. Each Palm Sunday the leftover palm branches were saved and burned. The following year, on Ash Wednesday, priests drew a cross with these ashes on the worshippers' foreheads and said, "Remember, O man, that thou art dust and unto dust shalt thou return" (from Genesis 3:19, King James Version).

Ashes have long been a symbol of repentance—turning from sin to God. The early Israelites mixed the ashes from their burnt offerings with water. Then they sprinkled this mixture over the unclean person (sinner) and his belongings as a sign of repentance (Numbers 19:17–18).

When the church began its ceremony, only sinners such as robbers and murderers received the ashes as a mark of their repentance. Later, perhaps out of sympathy, friends and relatives came with them and also received the ashes. Gradually, the ceremony began to include everyone in the church because "all have sinned; all fall short of God's glorious ideal" (Romans 3:23).

The weeks between Ash Wednesday and Easter are a time of preparation. In the early church those who were to be baptized on Easter used this time to study, pray, and fast. Strict fasting has nearly vanished, but some people still "give up something for Lent." It may be candy, ice cream, or dessert—but always something very important is given up for forty days. This small sacrifice is a reminder of the enormous sacrifice that Jesus made.

Today Lent is still a time to remember our sins and turn to

God for forgiveness. Some churches continue the practice of drawing a cross of ashes on worshippers' foreheads. Many have extra services. But all recognize these forty days as a special time of year to prepare Christians for Easter.

> Turn from your sins . . . turn to God . . . for the Kingdom of Heaven is coming soon.
> Matthew 3:2

LENT ACTIVITIES

Bulletin Board—LENT—40 DAYS OF PREPARATION

1. *background paper*
2. *construction paper*
3. *crayons, felt-tip pens, or colored pencils*

Draw pictures of what we do during Lent: Ash Wednesday services, "giving up something," praying, and attending worship services. Arrange on bulletin board.

FORTY DAYS OF PREPARATION

ASH WED. SERVICE•GIVING UP SOMETHING•KNEELING IN PRAYER•WORSHIP

Class Activity

Have the teacher burn a palm branch (or similar plant, paper or real) to ashes. Have students pair off and each place a cross of ashes on the forehead of the other. Discuss the meaning of the ashes and the significance of wearing them in a very obvious place. Also discuss why your church may or may not observe this custom.

Lenten Candle Devotions

1. *1 by 3 inch pine lumber,*
   63.5 centimeters (25 inches) long
2. *six purple candles*
3. *one white candle*

Cut the pine board to make two pieces, one 38 centimeters (15 inches) long, one 25.4 centimeters (10 inches) long. Form a cross and notch so the pieces lie flat. Drill seven holes; six to signify the wounds of Christ (feet, hands, side, head) and one hole in the center of the cross.

Use for classroom or family devotion time. During the first week's devotions, light all six purple candles. Each successive week extinguish one candle. Leave all candles dark from Good Friday to Easter day. On Easter Sunday light the white candle.

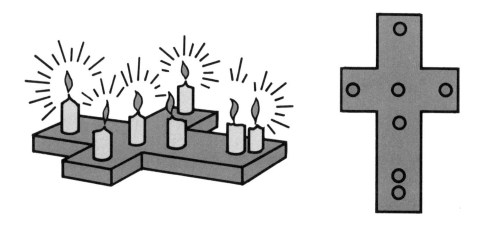

(Adapted from *Celebrations of Worship for the Church Year* by David Thompson and Mary Mergenthal, page 16. Copyright 1977, Augsburg Publishing House.Used by permission.)

Pretzel Activity

During Lent place a twisted pretzel on each family member's plate at a main meal. The pretzel was first made by monks in Europe as a reward for small children who remembered and said their prayers every day. These first pretzels were sweet and shaped to look like little arms folded in prayer.

Use the same shaped pretzels to remind your own family of

the importance of prayer. Have each family member fold his/her arms in the shape of a pretzel. Then say sentence prayers, pray silently, or join in a familiar family prayer.

Lenten Puzzle

The fourteen words listed below are hidden in this puzzle. Some of the words are spelled forward, backward, up, down, some at angles. The words to hunt for are:

spring	died	Lent	tomb
love	Son	Jesus	lily
cross	April	God	
church	save	soul	

```
J   W   A   D   L   X   B   C
E   F   P   E   E   G   M   H
S   P   R   I   N   G   O   U
U   W   I   D   T   K   T   R
S   Y   L   S   S   O   R   C
M   A   D   I   O   O   L   H
L   O   V   E   N   H   U   B
G   E   R   E   Y   L   I   L
```

(Contributed by Neva J. Korn)

Lent and You

Give up something for Lent that is important to you. Will it be something you do or eat? Discuss why.

6

HOLY WEEK

Holy Week is just what it sounds like—a week of holy events. Although it included a parade and a feast, it ended with Jesus' death on the cross.

The last week in Jesus' life began triumphantly. On Sunday during the Jewish Passover Jesus entered Jerusalem riding a donkey. Cheering crowds shouting "Hosanna!" lined the streets. Men, women, and children waved palm branches broken from the trees along the way. They threw them in His path. The people believed that Jesus was coming to overthrow their Roman rulers and set up His kingdom.

Today Christians relive that excitement and joy on Palm Sunday, the first day of Holy Week. Palms are placed throughout the church and sometimes given to worshippers. Like the hosannas which greeted Jesus, our joyful songs fill the air with praises to the Lord.

Christians all over the world observe Palm Sunday. But in England it is known as Olive Sunday, Branch Sunday, or Sunday of the Willow Boughs. In Germany the first day of Holy Week is called Blossom Sunday. Years ago, these places could not get palms for their services. So they used branches from trees in their own country. That is why their name for Palm Sunday is different from ours.

Monday, Tuesday, and Wednesday of Holy Week are quiet days for us. But in Jerusalem it was crowded and noisy. Thousands of people were there for the Passover. Many had seen Jesus' triumphant ride into the city and were eager to hear Him speak. So they followed Jesus and listened as He spent these three days teaching and preaching.

Wednesday was also the day that Judas made a deal with the chief priests. For thirty pieces of silver Judas agreed to betray the Master he had served and followed. Because of his evil deed, many people call this day Spy Wednesday.

The drama of Holy Week increases on Thursday. This was the last time Jesus and His disciples were together before His death. They gathered in the Upper Room for the Last Supper. While they ate, He told them to share bread and wine often as a way to remember Him. That same night Jesus washed the disciples' feet and His example teaches us that no one is too good to serve another. Then they left the Upper Room and went to the Garden of Gethsemane. There Judas betrayed Jesus by kissing Him on the cheek. Then the soldiers surrounded Jesus and took Him away.

In the fourth century the Thursday before Easter became known as Maundy Thursday. Services on this day include sharing bread and wine (communion) as Jesus and His disciples did at the Last Supper. The word *maundy* comes from the Latin word *mandatum* which means command. On that night long ago, Jesus said: "A new commandment I give unto you, That ye love one another; as I have loved you, that ye also love one another" (John 13:34, King James Version).

Holy Week's darkest moment came on Good Friday, probably called God's Friday in the early church. Today most churches mark this day with services from noon to three o'clock, the hours Jesus was nailed to the cross. He was thirsty and in terrible pain. All around Him people laughed, gambled for His clothes, and called Him names. Then He died. This was the saddest moment in all of God's creation.

The next day Mary, Mary Magdalene, the disciples, and all those who loved Jesus were heartbroken. Everything looked hopeless. Jesus was dead.

It is finished.

John 19:30

HOLY WEEK ACTIVITIES

Holy Week Mural

1. *paper for background*
2. *construction paper*
3. *crayons, felt-tip pens, colored pencils*

Divide paper into sections and draw pictures of the following events: (Draw directly on background or cut from construction paper.)
Palm Sunday—palms, parade
Monday and Tuesday—preaching and teaching
Wednesday—betrayal
Thursday—washing feet and Last Supper
Good Friday—on cross and death
Saturday—mourning
Easter!!

Passover Quiz
Since Easter began during the Jewish Passover, read the story of the first Passover in Exodus 12 or from a children's storybook Bible. Then complete the following quiz.
1. The Passover helps the Israelites (Jewish nation) remember that the _____ brought them out of _____ (verse 51).
2. Before the first Passover, God told _____ and _____ that this would be a memorial for the Israelites forever (verse 1).
3. Passover is celebrated each year by the Jewish nation for _____ days (verses 15 and 16).
4. The Passover began when the angel of death _____ _____ Israel's houses, because they had sprinkled _____ _____ on their doorposts and lintels (verse 13).
5. The lamb's blood saved the Israelites (all who believed and obeyed God) from _____ (verse 23).

6. _____ blood was shed on the cross to save _____ from death.

Answers to quiz:

3. seven	6. Jesus', us
2. Moses, Aaron	5. death
1. Lord, Egypt	4. passed over, lamb's blood

Talk Time
Discuss the meanings of the foods served during the Passover and emphasize that Jesus and His disciples ate these same foods at the Last Supper.
1. roasted shank bone of lamb = sacrifice of lamb
2. bitter herbs (such as horseradish) = bitterness of slavery
3. unleavened bread (matzah) = no time to raise and bake with leavening, running from Egypt
4. haroset (mixture of apples, nuts, raisins, and cinnamon) = mortar the Israelites had to use to mix bricks in Egypt
5. parsley and a roasted egg = greenery and renewal of life
6. salt water (to dip the egg and parsley in) = tears of the Israelite slaves

Role Play Activity
Read Matthew 27:11–55. Role play the last day in Jesus' life: trial, sentencing, crown of thorns and beating, walk to Calvary, crucifixion.
Discuss how each character involved must have felt: Jesus, soldiers, Pilate, crowd, Mary and followers, Simon (helped Jesus carry the cross).

Bulletin Board—CROSS SYMBOLS

1. *construction paper*
2. *writing paper*

Make construction paper crosses and place on the bulletin

board. Under each one write the meaning of the cross on another piece of paper. Examples:

THE LATIN CROSS—most widely used. The three steps represent faith, hope, and love.

THE PASSION CROSS—The pointed ends remind us of the points of the nails, thorns and spear that caused the suffering of Jesus.

CROSS OF GLORY—The rising sunrays behind the cross symbolize the new day when our Lord conquered death.

There are many more crosses!

Near Easter Sunday remove all other crosses and place the CROSS OF GLORY in the center of the bulletin board. Under it write "He is risen!"

(Contributed by Neva J. Korn)

43

Talk Time

> 1. *poster board*
> 2. *brown paint*
> 3. *plastic margarine dishes*

Discuss, or if alone, think about the bulletin board crosses (see above) and what they mean. Using poster board, draw and cut out the cross of your choice. Paint and let dry. Slit the bottom of an upside-down margarine dish and insert cross. Use to decorate your room or for a table centerpiece. Explain to your family what the cross means.

Hot Cross Buns

Ask your mother (or an older sister) to help you with this project. The recipe is as follows:

> *4 cups flour*
> *2 packages active dry yeast*
> *⅓ cup sugar*
> *¾ teaspoon salt*
> *½ teaspoon cinnamon*
> *¼ teaspoon nutmeg*
> *⅛ teaspoon cloves*
> *1¼ cups milk*
> *2 tablespoons butter or margarine*
> *2 eggs, lightly beaten*
> *1¼ cups raisins*
> *¼ cup diced candied orange peel or citron, optional*
>
> *Egg Glaze (1 egg, lightly beaten)*
> *Icing (recipe follows)*

In large mixing bowl combine 1½ cups of the flour, yeast, sugar, salt, and spices. In saucepan, warm the milk and butter to 130 degrees (bubbles appear around the edge of pan). Add to flour mixture. Beat 2 minutes at medium speed with electric mixer. Add eggs and ½ cup more flour; beat 2 minutes on high speed. Gradually stir in remaining 2 cups flour with raisins and peel. Knead on lightly floured board until smooth, about 5 minutes. Let rise in warm place in greased, covered bowl until double in size, about one hour. Punch down; divide into 18 equal parts. Shape into balls. Let rise in greased muffin pans* until doubled, about 45 to 60 minutes. Brush with egg glaze. Bake in 400 degree oven for 10 to 12 minutes, or until golden. Cool on rack. Drizzle icing over warm buns to form a cross. (Makes 1½ dozen buns.)

Icing: Beat smooth 1 cup confectioners sugar, sifted, and 2 tablespoons orange juice, lemon juice, or milk.

*Dough can also be baked in 6-ounce glass or foil custard cups.

(Recipe by Rachel Alfriend in *The Ledger-Star,* March 22, 1978—*The Virginian-Pilot,* March 23, 1978. Used by permission. Copyrighted.)

7
EASTER

For Christians, the most important holiday of the year is Easter. On this day Jesus rose from the dead. Because He died and came back to life, we know that death is not the end. We too will live forever.

"He is risen! He is risen! He is not dead! He lives!" The joyous shouts of Mary and Mary Magdalene shattered the early morning silence of that first Easter. The good news quickly spread from person to person. His followers were overjoyed.

From that time on, they celebrated His resurrection every year. Some kept the observance during the Jewish Passover, even though it came on a different day each year. But others celebrated it on a Sunday since that was the day Jesus came to life again. Because it was so confusing, in the year 325 Emperor Constantine, a Christian, called a meeting, the Council of Nicea. The men at this council decided that Easter should fall "upon the first Sunday after the first full moon after the twenty-first day of March." The full moon was important to light the way for pilgrims traveling to Jerusalem for Holy Week.

Also confusing is how we got the word "Easter." Some think it was the name of an early pagan goddess, Eostre. Her followers believed she opened the gates of spring and let the earth come alive again. When these people became Christians, it seemed natural to use her name for the time when Jesus came back to life. Others think Easter comes from the word "East" because the sun rises in the east, and Jesus was God's Son rising again. However the word came to us, it now means new life.

Over the years many customs became part of our Easter celebration. Perhaps the most inspiring is the sunrise service. The Bible says in Luke 24:1, "But very early on Sunday morning they took the ointments to the tomb . . ." Because of this, on Easter Sunday people of all ages gather at sunrise in cemeteries, on hilltops, or beside lakes to sing and praise God.

The custom of new clothes at Easter began years ago in the early church. Those people recently baptized dressed in white garments, while other church members wore new clothes as a remembrance of their own baptism. Therefore, new Easter outfits became a tradition, an outward sign of faith in the resurrection.

The Easter parade came from a procession held after church in many European countries. At the front of this procession was a large cross decorated with flowers and candles. As it passed through villages and countryside, mothers, fathers, boys, and girls hurried to join in. After hundreds of years, this religious walk still continues in some places. But in others it has become a parade to show off new Easter clothes.

Some customs are not directly related to the resurrection. One of the oldest is eating hot cross buns—sweet little buns topped with white icing crosses. The early Christians made them flat, or unleavened, like Passover bread. Later, they added fruits, and the buns became special sweet treats. In England and America they were so popular that men sold them on the streets by yelling, "One a penny, two a penny, hot cross buns."

The Easter bunny came to us, oddly enough, because of the moon. According to old Egyptian legends, the hare was a symbol of the moon. And since the moon is important in deciding the date of Easter, the hare became part of our celebration. Down through the years, the hare became the rabbit, and the rabbit became the bunny.

When we think of the Easter bunny, we also think of eggs. In ancient times eggs were symbols of spring, and people gave them to each other as gifts. But during Lent most Christians fasted and did not eat eggs. So on Easter, when the fast was over, one way they celebrated was by exchanging brightly colored eggs.

The parades, new clothes, bunnies, and eggs are fun and make us happy. But the happiness they bring is soon forgotten. Joy that will last forever is knowing that Jesus is alive today.

Everytime we see a cross, we know that Jesus fought death and won. The lamb reminds us that only His sacrifice can wipe away our sins. And the butterfly, one of the loveliest but less well-known Easter symbols, brings to mind new life.

New life—that is what Easter is all about. Without Jesus we would not have new life. He died. *But He did not stay dead.* He is stronger, more powerful than death. Because He lives, we live also—if we really believe.

> He isn't here! For he has come
> back to life again.
> Matthew 28:6

EASTER ACTIVITIES

Dogwood Legend

Obtain a real branch of dogwood if available or a picture of a dogwood flower. Look closely at the petals. Read the legend. Remember that it is only a legend, but the tree blooms in spring and the story ties in with the meaning of Easter—New Life.

Dogwood Legend

There is a legend that at the time of Jesus' Crucifixion the dogwood tree was one of the largest trees. It was so strong that it was chosen as the wood for the cross. The tree was deeply saddened by being used in this way. Jesus knew this as He was nailed to it. He said, "Because of your regret and pity for My suffering, never again shall the dogwood tree grow large enough to be used as a cross. Henceforth it shall be slender and bent and twisted and its blossoms shall be in the form of a cross." The flowers of the dogwood have two long and two short petals. In the center of the outer edge of each petal there is a dark stain. Some say it is the nail prints and stain of blood. The center of the flower looks like a yellow crown of thorns. All who see the dogwood flower should remember Jesus' death on the cross.

Easter Parade

Have an Easter Parade in your school or community. Make a cross from wood, or use heavy cardboard. Then decorate it with real or plastic flowers and candles, but do not light them. Form a procession with the cross at front. As the procession passes through school or neighborhood, sing "He Lives." If this is done in school, you can then use the cross as a decoration for your church, or donate it to a local orphanage or nursing home for others to enjoy.

Mock Stained-glass Windows

1. *black construction paper*
2. *various colors of cellophane*
3. *glue*

Talk about the Easter symbols. Obtain pictures of them or sketch them. Have each person choose a symbol and draw it on a piece of writing paper. Then sketch the same symbol very carefully on the black construction paper. Be sure to make all lines double so you can cut out the spaces for the cellophane. Cut out the areas in-between the double lines. Arrange and glue the colored cellophane to the back of the construction paper.

Talk Time

Greet everyone you meet on Easter Sunday with "He is risen!" Be ready to explain your greeting more fully. Keep a smile on your face.

Easter Cards

  1. *construction paper*
  2. *crayons, felt-tip pens, colored pencils*

Make Easter cards for shut-ins or someone lonely. Make them in a cross shape or egg shape. Fold a piece of construction paper in half. Begin on the fold line and sketch the desired shape. Cut, color, and decorate the front of the cards. Inside write: "He lives!" Happy Easter!

fold   cut line   fold   cut line

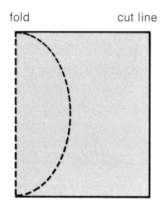 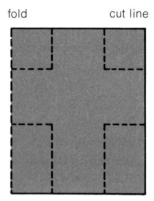

Butterfly Activity

  1. *white construction paper*
  2. *poster paint (various colors)*
  3. *pipe cleaners*

Fold the construction paper lengthwise. Draw out from the fold the shape of one butterfly wing. Cut it out and unfold the butterfly. Drop different colored paint in tiny drops on one of the wings. Fold again and press together so that the paint drops are absorbed on both sides. Open and let dry. Fold a pipe cleaner in half and put it on the top for the antenna.

Discuss the symbol for new life. The change from a caterpillar to a butterfly reminds us of the beautiful change our bodies will experience after we die.

fold

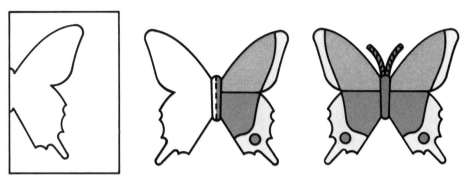

(Contributed by Emily Kast)

Cross Activity

> 1. *black construction paper*
> 2. *pictures of flowers (from magazines) or stickers*

Draw and cut out a cross from black construction paper. Find pictures of flowers in a magazine and cut them out or use stickers. Glue the flowers to the cross. The story has a sad beginning but a happy ending!

(Contributed by Emily Kast)

8
MOTHER'S DAY

God created Eve, the world's first mother, and the miracle of birth began. Since then, mothers everywhere have surrounded their children with warmth, tenderness, and love. On the second Sunday in May we say "thank you" to the one who brought us into God's world.

We love doing special things for Mother, like making her a surprise or washing the dishes before she asks. Anna M. Jarvis did something special too, for all mothers—she started Mother's Day.

Anna was born in Grafton, West Virginia, in 1864. Her mother cared for eleven children, taught Sunday School for twenty years, and delighted friends with gifts of flowers from her garden. To Anna, she was a shining example of love and unselfishness.

After Anna grew up and finished school, her family moved to Philadelphia. A few years later, Anna's mother died. As a tribute to her, Anna arranged special Mother's Day services in both the Grafton and Philadelphia churches which the family had attended.

This first Mother's Day was on Sunday, May 10, 1908. In both churches large jars of carnations, her mother's favorite flower, decorated the platform. Afterward, each person took one flower home as a remembrance. This led to the custom of wearing a carnation on Mother's Day. (A red or pink one means that your mother is living, and a white one means that she is dead.)

This tribute was so successful that Anna wanted a holiday for all mothers. She got her friends to help write letters. They wrote to ministers, businessmen, and congressmen all over America about Anna's idea.

Just three years after those first church services, every state had a day honoring mothers. Then on May 9, 1914, President Woodrow Wilson made Mother's Day a national holiday. He proclaimed it "a public expression of our love and reverence for the mothers of our country."

It wasn't long before other countries heard of Mother's Day. Now boys and girls in Denmark, Finland, Italy, Turkey, Australia, and Belgium honor their mothers on the second Sunday in May as we do. But in other countries children celebrate it on different days in different ways.

The English revived "Mothering Sunday," a very old holiday. On the fourth Sunday of Lent children give Mother a small gift, such as a trinket or wildflowers, and then the whole family attends church. Afterward, at a big feast, Mother is treated like a queen by everyone.

In France Mother's Day is the last Sunday in May. The entire family, from grandparents to babies, gathers for a big dinner. At the end of the meal, the children present Mother with a beautiful cake that looks like a bouquet of tiny flowers.

The Serbian people of Yugoslavia call their Mother's Day "Materice." It comes two weeks before Christmas. Early in the morning of "Materice," the children tiptoe into Mother's room and tie her up. When she awakens and sees herself all tied up, Mother begs the children to untie her. If they will, she promises to give them little gifts (fruits, toys, or clothes) which are hidden under her pillow.

In America mothers are honored in different ways also. Some see Mother's Day as a time for the whole family to be together, attend church, and share a special meal. Many children shower Mother with flowers, cards, and gifts. And everyone is saying, "I love you, Mom!"

We love Mother for many reasons, but one of the most important is her unselfishness. The Bible tells us about many mothers who put their children's well-being above their own feelings. One of the best examples of this comes from the book of 1 Kings 3:16–28.

Once two frantic women came to King Solomon. Each claimed the same baby belonged to her. Because Solomon did not know who the real mother was, he commanded a guard to cut the baby in two and give each woman half. One said, "Yes, that's fair." But the other cried, "NO! Give her the baby!" The real mother wanted the baby to live even if she had to give him up. Solomon knew this and gave the baby to her.

From the moment we are born, Mother loves us and cares for us. She finds our favorite toy in the place we just looked, stays by our side when we are sick, and teaches us how to talk to God with our first prayer. She sees the good in us when others don't and loves us through good times and bad. Because Mother is so special, we are proud to honor her on Mother's Day.

> Honor your ... mother, that
> you may have a long, good life.
> Exodus 20:12

MOTHER'S DAY ACTIVITIES

Recipe Holder with Love Recipe

1. *spray can lid*
2. *plastic fork*
3. *small plastic flowers*
4. *styrofoam cut to fit inside lid*
5. *small index cards*

Turn lid upside down, press styrofoam to the bottom. Insert fork handle into center of styrofoam. Arrange flowers around the fork.

On index card copy the following recipe:

1 can Obedience
1 pint Neatness
3 pints of Affection
1 can of Running Errands (Willing Brand)
1 cup of Pure Thoughtfulness
Dash of Holiday, Birthday, and Everyday Surprises
1 Box of Get Up When I Should (When Mother Calls Brand)
1 bottle of Keep Sunny All Day
Mix well, bake in a warm oven. Serve to Mother every day of the year in big slices.

Tissue Carnation

1. *red and white tissues*
2. *pinking shears*
3. *green pipe cleaners*

Cut folded part of tissue off. Fold remainder accordian fashion. Attach pipe cleaner around the middle of the tissue leaving end of pipe cleaner for stem. Clip ends of tissue with shears. Use pinking shears on some. Fluff. Add bow if desired. Make several and give to your mother for a Mother's Day bouquet.

IOU Basket

1. *construction paper*
2. *writing paper*
3. *felt-tip pens or pencil*

Make a basket of gifts that Mother, an aunt or elderly lady can use all year long. Draw the pattern on the construction paper. Cut and decorate the front using the words "IOU— (person's name)."

Then on the writing paper, list all the things you can do to help Mother (or another person) throughout the year. Cut each good deed out and fold it. Put them all in the basket. Examples: "Good for one weeding of the garden." "Good for one scrubbing of the bath tub." Try putting down deeds that are not your regular duties.

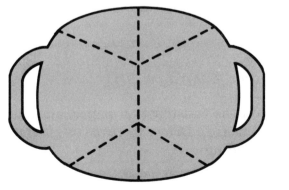

Enlarge pattern to approximately 15.2 centimeters (6 inches) by 22.8 centimeters (9 inches). Pattern on page 62.

(Contributed by Neva J. Korn)

Motherhood Mobile

1. *bleach bottle*
2. *string*
3. *pictures of Bible mothers (drawn or from magazines)*
4. *one picture of your mother (real or drawn)*
5. *construction paper*

Cut the top and bottom off the bleach bottle, leaving a plastic circle or ring. Attach different lengths of string to the circle with one long string tied to each side for hanging the mobile. Glue pictures to construction paper frames and label each. Tape to strings.

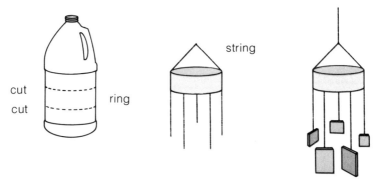

Bulletin Board—GOD MADE MOTHERS FOR . . .

1. *background paper*
2. *construction paper*
3. *crayons, felt-tip pens, colored pencils*

Draw large carnations on the construction paper, cut out, and arrange on bulletin board. Draw pictures of things mothers do. Place under headings:

creating (example, pictures of baby, sewing, crafts)
loving (example, pictures of hugging, reaching out)
caring (example, picture of sick child and mother)
teaching (example, picture of reading and praying)

Caring Card
Make and decorate a Mother's Day card for your mother.
Make another card for an elderly mother in your area who
lives alone. Deliver the card personally, if possible.

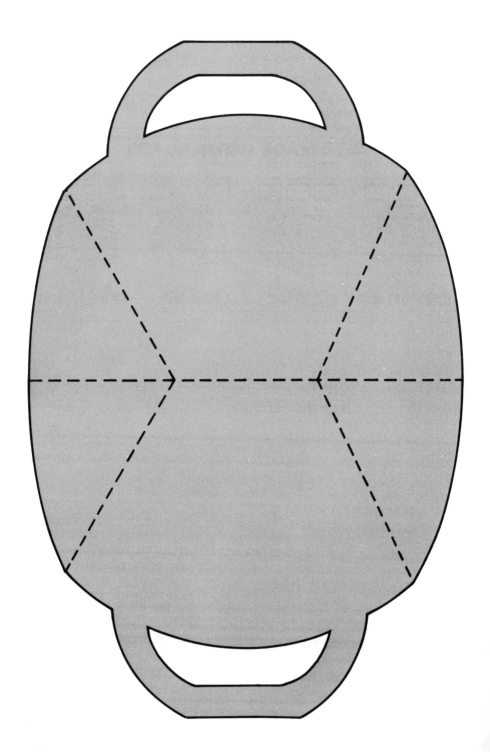

9

MEMORIAL DAY

On this day we remember the men and women who fought in wars for freedom in America and the world. Thousands died. So that their courage will not be forgotten, we honor them on the last Monday in May.

BOOM! BOOM! BOOM! A twenty-one gun salute rings through the air. The band stands rigidly at attention. A speaker's voice echoes in the air. Then relatives, friends, and strangers walk silently among the graves where tiny flags flutter. Some leave bouquets of flowers. Finally, a distant trumpeter plays the mournful tune of "Taps," and the ceremony ends.

Each Memorial Day such ceremonies honor those who died serving in the Army, Navy, Air Force, and Marine Corps. Flags also fly at half staff on all government buildings. And to remember those who died at sea, the Navy sets afloat tiny boats decorated with flowers.

The custom of decorating soldiers' graves began in 1865 after the Civil War. Brother fought brother, uncle fought nephew in the war between the Union (Northern States) and the Confederacy (Southern States). In memory of those who died, Henry C. Wells from Waterloo, New York, suggested that their graves be decorated with flowers.

The last Monday in May was chosen for this occasion which

eventually came to honor the dead from each of our wars, not just the Civil War. Although it was first named Decoration Day because of the decorated graves, all but a few southern states now call it Memorial Day. They instead celebrate Jefferson Davis's birthday (the president of the Confederacy) or Confederacy Memorial Day on different days in the spring. But whatever it is called, each state has set aside one day to remember all those who have died for our country.

Other countries have similar salutes to their war dead. Like America, they have also dedicated a tomb to those who died in their countries' wars but were never found or identified. This memorial in America is called the Tomb of the Unknown Soldier. It is located in the Arlington National Cemetery, Arlington, Virginia.

Even as we honor these brave men and women, it is our hope that peace will replace war forever. Adam and Eve lived peacefully in the Garden of Eden. Then sin entered the world bringing with it hate and greed. In a short time people took sides against each other. Fighting broke out. Soon there were wars. Whether the weapons were knives, bows and arrows, guns, or bombs, people died.

As Christians we must try to make friends of our enemies and share Jesus' love with them. Once the Prince of Peace reigns in a heart, He brings true justice and peace.

> Happy are those who strive for peace—they shall be called the sons of God.
>
> Matthew 5:9

MEMORIAL DAY ACTIVITIES

Role Play a Memorial Day Service
    If possible do this in a nearby cemetery. Perhaps some friend is a veteran and would be willing to come for this activity in uniform. Have your friends become the following people.
1. Characters: band, military, relatives, bystanders, minister.
2. "Taps" can be played on a record or by someone who can play the trumpet.
3. Place tiny flags and/or flowers on graves or places marked as graves.
4. Twenty-one gun salute from sound effects.
5. Minister speaks a few words.

Talk Time
    Include this activity with above or use separately.
1. Why did the people honored on Memorial Day die?
2. Do you know anyone from your family who died in a war?
3. Why do we have wars?
4. Will war ever stop? (Isaiah 2:2–4; Micah 4:3)
5. When?

Prayer Time
    Pray for real peace for our world. Using a map of the world, mark the countries where there is war going on now. Talk about the people and what war does to families. Pray for all concerned.

Navy Boats

1. *tiny plastic boats*
2. *styrofoam or clay*
3. *small plastic flowers*

Fill the boats with styrofoam or clay. Insert small plastic flowers to fill the boat. Keep as a reminder, or set them afloat on a lake or stream. As boats float away, remember all those who have died at sea in battles. Pray for their families.

Mural or Bulletin Board—PEACE→WAR→PEACE

1. *background paper*
2. *construction paper*
3. *crayons, felt-tip pens, colored pencils*

Divide the board into three sections and make large headings over each, PEACE→WAR→PEACE. Under the first heading, place a smaller title, Garden of Eden. Draw and color pictures of the garden and peace in the world. Under the second heading place the title, Fall of Man. Draw and color pictures of war: beginning with Cain and Abel to Armageddon (the last war). Under the third headline place the title, New World. These pictures should be of the Prince of Peace—Jesus—returning to the world bringing real peace.

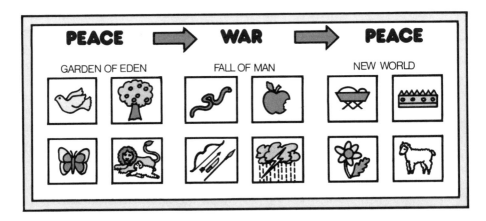

Memorial Bouquet

1. *construction paper*
2. *popsicle sticks*
3. *crayons, felt-tip pens, colored pencils*

Using the construction paper, make a small American flag and a cross. Color appropriately. Attach the flag to a popsicle stick by bending one end of the flag around the stick, tape or glue closed. Attach another popsicle stick to the bottom of the cross.

Pick a wildflower bouquet and place the flag and cross in the middle of the flowers. Give this to a person in your family or neighborhood who lost someone in a war or place it on the grave of a soldier. Pray for the family of a soldier.

10
FATHER'S DAY

Fathers have been important since God created Adam. They teach us, praise us, protect us, provide for us, and love us. This is a very big job! Because fathers are so important, we honor them with a special day, the third Sunday in June.

Everyone feels his own father is special: no one's shoulders are bigger for sitting on and watching parades; no one's arms are stronger for keeping us from harm; no one's handshake means more after a well-played ball game; and no one's smile is brighter as he hugs his little girl or boy.

Mrs. John Bruce Dodd of Spokane, Washington, believed her father was special too. He had raised six children alone after her mother's death. One Sunday morning in 1909, she listened to a sermon honoring mothers. "Why aren't fathers praised like mothers?" Mrs. Dodd wondered. "It isn't fair!"

So Mrs. Dodd asked a group of ministers to help arrange a day just for fathers. The next year on June 19 her wish came true. Spokane became the first city to officially honor fathers.

Soon her idea spread across America, and it became the only country which honored fathers with a day of their own. But it was only in 1972 that Congress made it permanent. Until then, this special day had to be declared each year by the President.

On this day we treat father like a king. Cards and gifts are brought out of hiding. Mother prepares his favorite dinner. Children place his newspaper and slippers beside his favorite chair. The whole family joins together to let father know how special he is.

The Bible tells us about many special fathers also. The most important, of course, is God. He is the One our fathers look to for strength and guidance. Even His Son, Jesus, prayed to Him often.

In the Old Testament (Genesis 22:1–13) we learn about Abraham, whose name means father of many nations. Abraham loved his son Isaac dearly. One day God tested his faith and obedience. He told Abraham to place Isaac on an altar and sacrifice him like a sheep. Abraham was shocked and torn between the deep love for his son and his belief that God was always right. In the end, he obeyed. But as he raised the knife, God stopped him. God did not want Abraham to hurt Isaac. God only wanted to see if Abraham would obey Him even when he did not understand. Abraham trusted his heavenly Father, and Isaac trusted Abraham.

In the New Testament (Luke 15:11–32) Jesus told the story of the prodigal son. The father in this story saw his son waste all his money and live like a pig. When the boy realized his mistakes, he wanted only to go home and live as a servant in his father's house. He did not feel worthy to be called a son. But his father welcomed him with a big party to show his love and forgiveness. He erased his son's mistakes just as God erases ours when we ask His forgiveness.

The word "father" is a title of honor. It is used sometimes for people who help create something important. For example, George Washington is called the father of America because he was so important to the birth of the nation.

We use the same title of honor for our father. After all, he helped create *us*. What could be more important than that?

Father also sets an example for his children. He teaches us to stand up for our beliefs but still see the other side. By loving us even when we do wrong, he shows us in a small way just how much God loves all His children. He is always there when we need him. Even his discipline prepares us to obey teachers, the law, and especially God.

Yes, father is special. If we love and appreciate him, God is happy and blesses us.

> Honor your father . . . that you
> may have a long, good life.
> Exodus 20:12

FATHER'S DAY ACTIVITIES

Father's Day Quiz

God the F _ _ _ _ _

_ _ A _

_ _ _ _ T _ _ _

_ _ H _

_ _ _ E _

_ _ R _ _ _ _

Answer the following questions and fill in above:

F. We are His children (1 Corinthians 8:6).

A. The father who built a boat and saved his family (Genesis 6:12–22).

T. He died in battle for his father, King Saul (1 Samuel 14:6–15; 31:2).

H. God caused his father to lose his voice till he was born (Luke 1:12–20).

E. The father who led his people out of Egypt (Exodus 3:1–10).

R. The father of many nations (Genesis 17:4–6).

Answers to quiz: F. Father; A. Noah; T. Jonathan; H. John; E. Moses; R. Abraham.

(Contributed by Neva J. Korn)

Make a Father's Day Card

1. *construction paper*
2. *crayons, felt-tip pens, colored pencils*

Fold paper in half and draw a picture on the front. Inside write a picture story about the things you like to do best with your father. Do this by using "U" for you; draw an eye for "I," etc. For example:

love U
because U take me  !

 love U
! because U take me to  !

Home Activity

Jesus taught His disciples to wash each other's feet (John 13:5). As a special token of love for your father, polish his shoes! Leave a note in the shiny shoes telling how much you love him.

(Contributed by Florence W. Pauls)

Cookie Canister

1. *coffee can*
2. *felt (2 colors)*
3. *glue*
4. *cookies, brownies, or candy*
5. *construction paper*
6. *crayons, felt-tip pens, colored pencils*

Wrap the entire coffee can with a large piece of felt cut to fit. Decorate it with additional felt scraps cut in sports shapes (golf club, fishing pole, baseball glove and bat) or designs a man would like.

Ask mom to help you make a batch of cookies, brownies, or candy. Fill the coffee can with the cooled treats.

Make a Father's Day card with construction paper. Glue felt sports shapes on front of card. Color and decorate inside. Give the cookie canister and card to your grandfather, uncle, or some elderly man.

Bulletin Board—GOD MADE FATHERS TO ...

1. *background paper*
2. *construction paper*
3. *crayons, felt-tip pens, colored pencils*

Draw large sports shapes on the construction paper; such as a basketball, football, bat, tennis racket. Cut out and place on the bulletin board. Have classmates draw pictures of things fathers do for us. Place under these headings: TEACH—DISCIPLINE—LOVE—PROTECT—PROVIDE.

11
BIRTHDAYS

Your birthday is special because it celebrates the birth of a person unlike any other in all of God's creation—YOU!

HAPPY BIRTHDAY! The cake sparkles with candles, flashbulbs pop brightly, and gaily wrapped presents wait to be opened. This is your very own holiday!

A birthday is extremely important. Without one you would not be alive. It is your beginning. It also determines when you start school, when you are old enough to vote, and when you legally become an adult.

Many things can happen on this special day. A party may await you at school, the ice cream parlor, or in your home. Friends may surprise you with something special. Or perhaps Mom will cook your favorite dinner.

You are the center of all this attention because you are very special. *You are different from every other person in the world.* No one else talks like you, walks like you, or looks like you. And yet God knows every single thing about you. He knows the exact number of hairs on your head (Luke 12:7)! God knows when you sit. He knows when you stand. He even knows what you are thinking before you say it (Psalm 139)!

God knows all this because He created you. And when you were born, God ordered His angels to watch over you the rest of your life (Psalm 91:11). That is how important you are to Him, and that is why He gave you this special day.

> May the Lord bless and protect you; may the Lord's face radiate with joy because of you.
>
> Numbers 6:24–25

BIRTHDAY ACTIVITIES

Spin the Bottle

Use any bottle with a narrow neck. Have boys and girls sit in a circle with the birthday person in the middle. Have children take turns spinning the bottle. The person it points to must say one good thing about the birthday child before he/she counts to the new age. (Stress character-building qualities.) If the person doesn't answer within the count, then that child is out for the remainder of the game. Continue until only one child and the birthday person are left. A small award can be given the winner.

(This activity will help children to see good qualities in everyone!)

Birthday Crown (younger children)

>   1. *poster board*
>   2. *aluminum foil*
>   3. *paint or felt-tip pens*

Teacher, parents, or friends can make a crown from poster board. Write "I am God's child" across the crown and decorate it with drawings of gems and stars. Gems can be cut from aluminum foil. Cut, fold in a circle, and staple in the back. The birthday child can wear this all day at home or school.

Birthday Shield (older children)

>   1. *sheet of construction paper or poster board*
>   2. *crayons, felt-tip pens or colored pencils*

Draw and cut the paper in the shape of a shield. Put your last name at the top. Divide the bottom portion into four parts. Using symbols, drawings, and words describe yourself. Use one space for your favorite hobby, another for what or who you love the most, career plans, and a picture or drawing of yourself.

Fingerprint Picture

   1. *light-colored construction paper*
   2. *ink pad*
   3. *magnifying glass*

Press thumb, fingers, and base of hand onto the ink pad. Then carefully press prints onto the construction paper. Copy the following poem under the picture.

I have four fingers and one thumb,
My hand is just like yours, you see.
But one thing God made quite clear,
My fingerprints belong to me.

Look at prints through a magnifying glass. Discuss that each picture is unique—because you are!

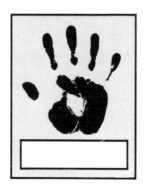

Birthday Present Quiz

We look forward to our birthdays because we receive gifts from our family and loved ones. God has given us many good gifts also. They are wrapped up in His Word. Can you find six of them?

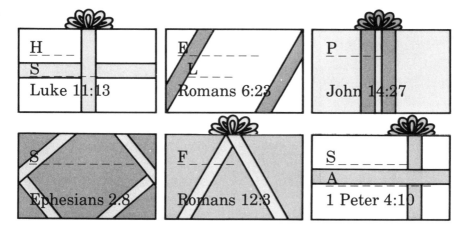

Answers: Holy Spirit, eternal life, peace, (saved) salvation, faith, special abilities.

(Contributed by Neva J. Korn)

12
INDEPENDENCE DAY

The Fourth of July is America's most important patriotic holiday. As flags flutter proudly in the wind, fireworks burst forth in the red, white, and blue colors of America. This is the birthday of the United States of America, land of the free, home of the brave, one nation under God.

Pretend for a moment that you do not live in a free country such as America. You are grown up and want to be a teacher, but the government says you must become a doctor. You tell the truth about an important person, and the police put *you* in jail. You want to visit another country, but the guards refuse to let you leave. Your freedom is gone.

Freedom was the main reason that America became a country. Beginning with the Pilgrims, thousands of people journeyed to America seeking freedom to worship God and to live by the plan given in the Bible.

But while the people were free to worship God, England still made the laws for the new country. After many years, the American people decided to rule themselves. So on July 4, 1776, men from each of the thirteen colonies announced to the world that the United States of America was a free and separate country. This was the Declaration of Independence.

Of course, that was just the beginning. The colonists had to fight a long, hard war to win that independence—the Revolutionary War. After it ended, the Fourth of July was the one day that symbolized all the struggles of that fight for freedom.

The day after the forefathers declared their independence, John Adams (the second President of the United States) wrote a letter to his wife. As strange as it may seem, he said, "July, 1776 . . . will be celebrated by succeeding generations . . . with pomp and parade, with shows, games and sports, guns, bells, bonfires, and illuminations from one end of this continent to the other, from this time forward, forevermore . . . ." As we all know, his prediction came true.

The first Independence Day celebration took place in Philadelphia in 1777. Ships in the harbor fired thirteen-gun salutes (one for each colony), houses in the city sparkled with candlelight, bells rang, bonfires raged, and fireworks exploded in the sky.

The celebrations are to remember the many people who fought to make America free. One was George Washington who is called the father of the country. As a general, Washington led the fight for freedom and later became the first President. Although we do not hear much about Washington's faith in God, he went to church regularly, read his Bible, and cared for the needy in his community. When he became the first President, an oath (promise) was written for him to repeat. At the end of it, Washington himself added, "So help me God."

To help Americans remember freedom all through the year, America has many symbols—the bald eagle, the Statue of Liberty, the flag, and Uncle Sam. But one of its most precious is the Liberty Bell. Most people know it has a crack in it, some know it was made in England, but few realize the words around it come from the Bible. "Proclaim liberty throughout the land unto all the inhabitants thereof" (Leviticus 25:10).

Even the motto of America, "In God We Trust," shows that the nation depends on God to help keep freedom. He tells us in Romans 13:1–2 to "obey the government, for God is the one who has put it there ... those who refuse to obey the laws of the land are refusing to obey God ...."

Since God has planned the government, it must please Him to see His children working together. The celebrations of America's birthday must please God too. When we celebrate we are saying "thank you" to those who fought for our freedom. But above all, we are praising God for such a beautiful land and His many blessings on it.

> Praise the Lord, all nations everywhere. Praise Him, all the peoples of the earth. For he loves us very dearly, and his truth endures. Praise the Lord.
>
> Psalm 117

INDEPENDENCE DAY ACTIVITIES

Flag Activity

> 1. *poster board*
> 2. *white construction paper*
> 3. *popsicle (craft) sticks*
> 4. *crayons, felt-tip pens, colored pencils*

Use real flags or make large poster board flags (one American and one Christian) for display in your classroom or home.

Make small flags by cutting construction paper into 6 by 10 centimeters (2½ by 4 inch) pieces. Fold 1 centimeter (½ inch) from left side. Draw and color the flags. Glue a popsicle stick inside the fold.

Talk Time

With your newly made flags in front of you, discuss the following:

1. What is a flag?
2. Why is the United States flag held in such high esteem?
3. How many flags do you honor? (U.S., Christian, state, scout, etc.)
4. How many different flags has America had? Why? Can you draw some of them?

Pledges

Learn and recite the pledge of allegiance to the United States flag and the Christian flag. Discuss what they mean.

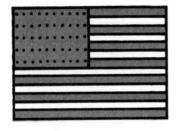

I pledge allegiance to the flag of the United States of America and to the Republic for which it stands, one Nation under God, indivisible, with liberty and justice for all.

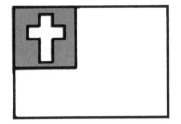

I pledge allegiance to the Christian flag, and to the Savior for whose kingdom it stands, one brotherhood, uniting all mankind in service and love.

Bulletin Board or Individual Project

1. *background paper*
2. *poster board*
3. *construction paper*
4. *crayons, felt-tip pens, colored pencils*

Use poster board for the bulletin board, construction paper for individual project. Divide paper in half with crayon or felt-tip marker line. In the upper left-hand corner draw a United States flag. To the right of the line, draw a Christian flag. Write across the top, "Render therefore unto Caesar the things that are Caesar's (divide here) unto God the things that are God's" (Matthew 22:21, King James Version).

Using construction paper, draw pictures of things for God in one column and things for government in the other column. For example, under the left side you might show paying taxes, on the right side giving tithes (offerings) at church. Label each picture.

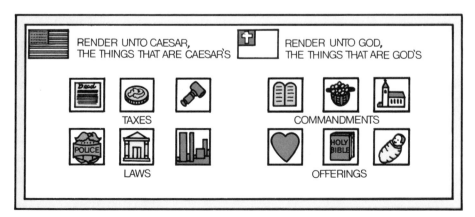

Role Play Activity

Role play situations in which we have freedom and others don't. For example the three situations in paragraph two of this chapter.

Independence Day Picnic

Plan a picnic. In your decorations use the Christian and American flags together. Make a birthday cake with "God Bless America" on top and sing "Happy Birthday" to America. Pray for America by praying for the President, the governor of a state, the mayor of a city, and all others in authority (1 Timothy 2:1–2). Ask God for peace.

13
LABOR DAY

God gave everyone talent, the ability to do certain things well. Labor Day honors those who work and use their talents. We celebrate it the first Monday in September.

Early one morning a young boy watched his friends hurry off to school. Then shrugging his shoulders, he clutched his lunch bag and headed for the big factory. There he worked long, hard hours for very little money. This boy was Peter J. McGuire, the founder of Labor Day.

Peter was born in New York City in 1858. He had nine brothers and sisters. Because his family was poor, Peter had to work to help buy food and clothes. As he grew up, he realized how unsafe the machinery and buildings were for the men who worked there. But like Peter, they had to work under those conditions to support their families. The courage and determination of these men impressed Peter very much.

So in 1882 he asked a labor union in New York City to honor America's workers with a holiday on the first Monday in September. He picked this day because it came between Independence Day and Thanksgiving, a good time for a break. The union decided to try his idea.

Their first celebration took place in New York City on September 5, 1882. Ten thousand people paraded through the streets. Then they gathered for a huge picnic of salads, sandwiches, and pies. Afterward, the workers talked about a better future and listened to speakers praise them. Finally, to top off the event, fireworks lit up the sky. The day was so successful, everyone wanted to repeat it the next year.

Soon other cities began their own celebrations. On February 21, 1887, Oregon became the first state to officially recognize Labor Day. By September 3, 1934, all the states had agreed to honor workers on this day.

It did not take long for Labor Day to become a family day as well as a salute to America's workers. It is the last big summer holiday, the end of school vacation. People still parade and picnic, but they celebrate in other ways too. Some go to the beach and splash in the waves one last time. Others attend baseball games or just stay home and do nothing. They rest from labor.

Celebrating is fun, but God has work (labor) for us to do too. He gave all of us different talents, each important in its own way. Just as each part of our body has a job (our eyes see, our hands touch, our feet walk), so do the workers in God's world. Without carpenters we would not have houses; without teachers we would not learn to read; and without farmers we would not have food. Everyone has a job to do.

The Bible tells us that God works too. "In the beginning God created the heaven and the earth" (Genesis 1:1, King James Version). But that was not the end of His labor. Today He is busy healing the sick, teaching us right from wrong, and answering our prayers (yes, no, or wait).

Even Jesus learned a trade. The gentlest man on earth— preacher, teacher, and Son of God—was a carpenter. As a young boy He learned from Joseph how to work with wood and make things with His hands.

Jesus' followers were also hard workers. Peter was a fisherman. Luke was a doctor. Paul was a tentmaker. Mary and Martha were homemakers. They used their jobs to help themselves and others.

Like them, we must put our talents to work. God expects us

to use them wisely and do a good job. No matter what He calls us to be—ballplayer, teacher, astronaut—if we do our best, we please Him. So on Labor Day we salute those who use their God-given talents to make His world better.

> Six days a week are for your daily duties and your regular work.
>
> Exodus 20:9

LABOR DAY ACTIVITIES

Bulletin Board—"CALL GOD AT WORK"

1. *background paper*
2. *construction paper*
3. *black yarn*
4. *crayons, felt-tip pens, colored pencils*

Make a *large* telephone receiver from black construction paper. Place the receiver at the top of the bulletin board, and make a cord with black yarn to wind from top to bottom. Print a large headline at the top of the board: "CALL GOD AT WORK." Under this headline, make three smaller headlines: His number is Jeremiah 33:3 (King James Version); His answer is "Call unto me, and I will answer ..."; His business is: creating, healing, teaching, etc.

Under the last headline, divide the board into three sections. Have classmates draw and color pictures about the work God does, such as giving us doctors and friends, supplying energy and food, and giving us His Spirit to help understand the Bible.

Worker's in God's World Mobile

1. *balloon*
2. *papier-mâché (strips of paper, bowl of half glue and half water)*

3. poster paint
4. string
5. construction paper

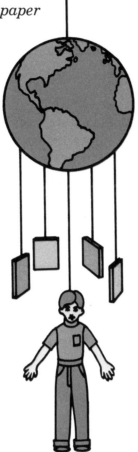

Blow up the balloon and tie a long string onto the end for hanging the mobile. Cover with papier-mâché by dipping strips of paper in mixture of water and glue and placing on balloon. Let dry. Use masking tape and attach different lengths of string onto the dried papier-mâché, with one long string centered. Paint entire ball blue, let dry. Paint countries or cut out pictures and glue onto the papier-mâché to make it look like a globe.

On pieces of construction paper 7.6 by 12.7 centimeters (3 by 5 inch), draw or glue on pictures of people working. Make a hole in the top of each with a paper punch or scissors and tie string through hole. The center string should be for a large figure of a human. Emphasize on the figure the eyes (to see), the hands (to work), the ears (to hear), the feet (to walk). All are essential to the body, everyone is essential to God's world.

Talk Time
Read 1 Corinthians 12:12–26.
Have some simple jigsaw puzzles for classmates to put together, but *remove one* piece from each. When they have all discovered that pieces are missing, discuss how each part of our body contributes to the whole and how each worker contributes to the whole. Like a jigsaw puzzle, each piece fits together, and when one is missing the picture is incomplete.

Plan a Labor Day Picnic
Plan a family, church, or community picnic. Decorate the tables with different tools for different occupations, for example, books and pencils for teachers, doctor kit, tools for carpenter, etc.
After the picnic have a speech, debate, or discuss how different talents are equally important. If possible, note each person's contribution to the family, community or church. A good starting point might be to read Psalm 127:1, "Unless the Lord builds a house, the builders' work is useless. Unless the Lord protects a city, sentries do no good."

What Is Your Talent?
Everyone is good at something: drawing, singing, writing, making people feel good, cleaning, yard work, crafts. What is your talent? Use it to brighten someone's day!

14
HALLOWEEN

Halloween is a spooky time of year. Costumes, masks, and skeletons appear everywhere. We make bats, cats, witches, and jack-o'-lanterns out of black and orange paper. But the world "Halloween" really means holy evening.

The night is crisp, and the moon is full. The wind howls. There is a rap on the door. It c-r-e-a-k-s open.
"TRICK-OR-TREAT!"
Halloween has been a goose-bumpy night for thousands of years. But it hasn't always been called Halloween. Long before the time of Jesus, people called Celts lived in France, England, Ireland, and Scotland. They did not know about God.

Instead, they worshipped the sun-god who ruled the summer and Saman (Sah' win), the god of death, cold, and darkness, who ruled the winter. As summer ended, the Celts believed that Saman was attacking the sun-god. They didn't know that the earth moved around the sun causing the seasons to change. They were afraid the sun would be gone forever.

To help their sun-god stay alive, the Celts held a ceremony called Samhain (Sah' win) each year at the end of October. They built big fires on the hilltops to strengthen their dying god and to frighten away the evil spirits. They also sacrificed crops and animals to Saman hoping to please him enough so that he would let the sun live.

At this same time of year, the Romans also had a festival. They called it Pomona Day in honor of Pomona, their goddess of fruits and gardens. During this holiday the people laid out vegetables, nuts, and fruits (especially apples) to thank Pomona for a good harvest.

Then in the first century, the Romans conquered Britain. As they lived among the Celts, the customs of Samhain and Pomona mixed. But this holiday was not yet called Halloween.

When Christianity spread across Europe and Britain, the church taught that the earth was ruled by God—not by the sun, the darkness, or Pomona. To take the place of these superstitious festivals, in the year 835 the church made November 1 a Christian holiday. All Hallow's Day (also called All Saints' Day) was to honor all the saints who had no special day of their own. The night before All Hallow's Day became All Hallow's Even, meaning holy evening. Later, it was shortened to Halloween.

On All Hallow's Day the churches displayed relics (clothes, books, papers) that had belonged to or were about their saints. But the poorer churches could not afford these prized items. So some people dressed up as saints and paraded around the churchyard. Others made costumes of angels or devils and joined the parade. Even before Christianity, the Celts had dressed as evil spirits to please Saman. From these two ancient practices came our custom of dressing up on Halloween.

After the great potato famine in the 1840s, hundreds of Irish came to America. They brought with them one of our favorite Halloween customs—the jack-o'-lantern. In Ireland children used to hollow out a turnip, carve a grinning face on it, and put a lighted candle inside. In America they discovered the pumpkin. It was bigger, more colorful, and made a much better jack-o'-lantern.

The jack-o'-lantern legend tells us there once lived a very stingy boy named Jack. He died and went to the gates of heaven but couldn't get in. Then he headed for the gates of hell. But the devil didn't want him either because Jack had tricked him once. So the devil threw a hot coal from his fires at Jack. Instead of hitting him, the coal landed in the turnip he was munching on. This became Jack's lantern as he walked the earth forever in search of a resting place.

In America Halloween became a night for bonfires, dunking for apples, taffy pulls, popping corn, telling ghost stories, and trick-or-treating. Pranksters darted from house to house switching house numbers and street signs. They put wagons on top of barns and rocking chairs in trees. This was all done in fun. But to keep from being tricked, people started giving treats to the pranksters. Soon children everywhere were happily shouting, "Trick-or-treat!"

Although Halloween began in other countries, today it is mainly celebrated in America. However, American children have found a way to share it once again with the world. In 1950 a small Sunday School class decided to share instead of scare. So they rang doorbells and collected $36.00 in pennies. They sent this money to UNICEF (United Nations' International Childrens' Emergency Fund). Now church youth groups and school children carry the orange and black cartons which say, "Trick-or-Treat for the World's Children."

This holiday that began in fear and terror has turned into a day of fun and merry making. Although it is a delightful time of year, Halloween reminds us that people long ago believed in evil spirits. But today some people think these spirits are not real.

As Christians, we know the devil and his helpers *are* real. The Bible tells us they are at war with God. They fear Jesus because His power is the only thing that can defeat them.

Angels are very real also. They are busy guarding and protecting us, because we are right in the middle of the battle. God tells us to fight against the devil and his army (Ephesians 6:12). It is hard! But when we become a Christian soldier, we join the mightiest army in God's creation. With the angels, we will follow Jesus to victory!!

> Now you don't need to be afraid of the dark any more . . . the evil will not touch me . . . I choose the God above all gods to shelter me.
>
> Psalm 91:5–9

HALLOWEEN ACTIVITIES

Jesus—the Light of the World
Have small flashlights or penlights, one for each person if possible. Find a completely dark area—a closet, room. Form a circle with teacher or parent in the middle.

1. With all lights off, discuss how the Celts must have felt when they believed the sun was dying.

2. We know the Celts thought they were helping the sun, but did their ceremony really keep the sun alive?

3. Who has always controlled the sun?

4. Have someone quote Genesis 1:3, "And God said, Let there be light." Then have the person turn on his/her light. (Emphasize that God has always controlled the sun.)

5. Quote John 8:12, Jesus said, "I am the light of the world." Now discuss that the true light, Jesus Christ, has always been with us, but not everyone (then and now) recognizes Him as this true Light of the World.

6. The Bible tells us that everyone must let the light of Jesus shine through them. Sing "This Little Light of Mine" as each person turns on his light.

7. Have someone emphasize that lights can be turned off, the sun goes down, etc. But Jesus, the Light of the World, never goes out. He is always with us. His light is the only thing that can chase the rulers of darkness away.

Make a Candle

1. *pint milk carton*
2. *melted down candles or household wax*
3. *pipe cleaner*
4. *birthday or votive candle, 4 inches high*
5. *small card inscribed with John 8:12*

Open top of milk carton and pull out even with sides. Make a tiny hole in one side of the carton. Insert the pipe cleaner through the hole and glue the inscribed card onto the end of the pipe cleaner. Melt the old candles or household wax. Bits of old candles or crayons will add color. Place the regular candle in the middle of the carton. Pour hot wax into carton. Let sit until cool, then peel off the milk carton.

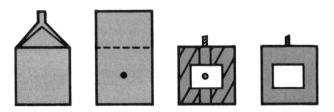

All Hallow's Celebration

Reread the portion of this chapter dealing with the beginning of All Hallow's Day. Discuss who saints are. (All believers are saints: Acts 9:13, 32, 41; Acts 26:10; Romans 1:7.)

Plan an All Hallow's Day parade. Paraders can dress as their favorite saints. (Since all true believers are saints, paraders may choose one from the Bible or someone they know—grandmother, minister, missionary, uncle, etc.) They must be prepared to share who they are and why they chose that person. Parade around school or neighborhood.

Trick-or-Treat Sharing

Save a portion of your trick-or-treat candy. Share with a local orphanage where the boys and girls are not able to trick-or-treat. Sick children and very young children do not go trick-or-treating. Share your treats with them.

Jack-o'-Lantern

Get a real pumpkin. Carve the stem out with a circle shape. Make hole large enough so that you can reach in and get all the seeds out. Cut a happy face on the pumpkin to remind us that we are safe with Jesus inside of us. Place a candle to represent Jesus, our light, inside. We need never experience complete darkness inside. Bake the seeds with a little salt and a little oil. Let the baked seeds cool and then enjoy eating your snack.

(Contributed by Emily Kast)

Bulletin Board—SPIRIT WARS

1. *background paper*
2. *construction paper*
3. *crayons, felt-tip pens, colored pencils*

   Make a large set of scales, large enough to cover the entire bulletin board. On the lighter side of the scales write—Satan and demons. On the heaviest side write—Jesus and angels. Students can draw Satan (Lucifer) being cast from heaven (Isaiah 14:12–15) and ways the devil tempts us—stealing, cheating, fighting. Place these under Satan and demons. Under Jesus and angels, place pictures of Jesus, guardian angels, messenger angels, and draw pictures of ways angels help (see "Angel Quiz" which follows).

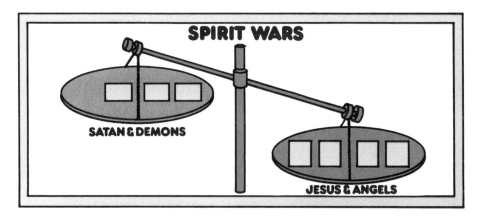

Angel Quiz
   1. Were angels present when the earth was made? (Job 38:7)
   2. Who made the angels? (Psalm 148:2, 5)
   3. Do angels have names? (Daniel 10:13; Luke 1:19)
   4. Do angels have feelings? (Luke 15:10)
   5. Do angels die? (Luke 20:36)
   6. Where do angels live? (Matthew 18:10)
   7. Do angels know as much as God? (Matthew 24:36)
   8. How many angels are there? (Luke 2:13)

9. Do we ever see angels? (Hebrews 13:2)
10. What do angels do? (Revelation 21:12; Hebrews 1:13–14; Psalm 91:11; Luke 2:13; Matthew 4:11)

Answers to quiz: 1. yes   2. God   3. yes   4. yes
5. no   6. heaven   7. no   8. multitude-innumerable
9. yes   10. guard gates; spiritual messengers; guardians; praise God; minister to and care for Jesus and us.

15
THANKSGIVING

Children dressed as Pilgrims and Indians remind us of America's first Thanksgiving. This holiday has always been a time for grandparents, aunts, uncles, cousins, and friends to gather for a big feast of turkey and all the trimmings. On this day Christians say "thank you" to God for all blessings.

As Father carves the big juicy turkey, Mother lights the candles on the dining room table. And the children dare each other to poke a finger in the cranberry sauce. Everyone is hungry and ready for the feast.

Delicious smells and tasty foods have always been part of thanksgiving celebrations. Unlike other holidays, the idea for this family day began with God. He told Moses that the Israelites were to observe a festival called the Feast of Booths. It was to be a time of thanksgiving for a good harvest and a reminder of the way they had lived in the wilderness. So they built tiny booths out of palm fronds, willow switches, and leafy branches, then decorated them with fruits and vegetables. For the seven days of this happy festival, families lived and feasted in these booths.

Down through the years people everywhere have celebrated good harvests. But Thanksgiving Day is strictly an American holiday which began with the Pilgrims. The Pilgrims were a group of Christians who lived in England and were persecuted for many years. So in 1608 they moved to Holland. Even though the Dutch people made them welcome, the Pilgrims did not feel at home. After twelve years they decided to travel to America and build a new life.

On September 6, 1620, a ship named the Mayflower sailed from England. The Pilgrims were among 102 passengers crowded on board to make the long, dangerous journey across the ocean. For sixty-six days the ship rolled and tossed. Finally, it reached a harbor. Safe at last, the Pilgrims stepped onto Plymouth Rock.

It was almost winter, so they began building houses and storerooms right away. They needed a place to keep their food dry during the rain and snow. They also needed shelter for everyone, especially those who were sick from the voyage. By the end of that horrible winter, almost half of them were dead.

When spring came, the brave Pilgrims welcomed the warm breezes and new hope. At that time they also met a very special Indian friend. His name was Squanto.

Squanto was a big help to the busy Pilgrims. They learned to catch fish and wild game the Indian way. He showed them how to plant corn, pumpkins, and beans. He even taught them which plants to use for medicine. The Pilgrims had a governor named Bradford who said that Squanto "was a special instrument sent of God for their good."

From time to time other Indians appeared in the distance. They had bows, arrows, and painted faces. When the Pilgrims tried to make friends with them, they darted back into the woods. So Squanto brought their chief, Massasoit, to meet the Pilgrims. They too became friends and signed a peace treaty which lasted fifty-five years.

In October of 1621, the harvest was so good that Governor Bradford suggested a celebration. The Pilgrims invited their friends, the Indians, to join them. The men hunted turkey, deer, duck, and geese.

On the morning of the celebration the Pilgrims gathered to worship God and thank Him for their many blessings. Large kettles of soups and vegetables bubbled over the fires, and meats roasted slowly on spits. When everything was ready, the women filled long tables with lobsters, oysters, fish, eels, white bread, corn bread, biscuits, Indian pudding, and pies.

Then Chief Massasoit arrived with ninety braves, and the three-day feast began. Between meals, the Pilgrims and Indians played games, wrestled, and ran races. It was truly a time of friendship and thankfulness.

As America grew, the colonists moved on across the land carrying with them the custom of thanksgiving. Then in 1789 George Washington proclaimed the first nationwide Thanksgiving Day to celebrate America's freedom from England. But after that one big holiday, people went back to observing the custom at different times and in different ways.

Nearly forty years later, a New England woman began a campaign to make Thanksgiving Day a national holiday. Mrs. Sarah Hale, the editor of a popular ladies' magazine, strongly believed that Americans should once again celebrate Thanksgiving Day together. She wrote articles in her magazine and letters to governors and presidents urging their help.

On October 3, 1863, Mrs. Hale's dream came true. President Abraham Lincoln invited her to the White House and issued his Thanksgiving Proclamation. This made it a national holiday to be held the last Thursday in November. (November sometimes has five Thursdays. So in 1941 Congress changed Thanksgiving Day to the fourth Thursday.)

Today we gather as the Pilgrims did with family and friends to worship, share an abundant feast, and play games. But in this modern world of supermarkets and TV dinners, it is easy to forget that our food is still the result of a good harvest. Everything we have comes from God, and we should thank Him every day.

God commanded His chosen people, the Israelites, to celebrate their harvest with the Feast of Booths. We too are His people, and Thanksgiving Day is our special time to say "thank you" to Him for *all* our blessings.

> Let your lives overflow with joy and thanksgiving for all he has done.
>
> Colossians 2:7

THANKSGIVING ACTIVITIES

Feast of Booths Activity

> *1. very large cardboard box (from appliance store)*
> *2. tree branches or willow switches*
> *3. plastic fruit, vegetables, baskets*

Cut out one side of the box leaving the top and three sides. Attach the branches to the outside to make it look like a booth. Decorate with plastic fruit, vegetables, and baskets.

With booth completed, read Leviticus 23:33–44. Act out this very early thanksgiving celebration.

Bulletin Board—ALL THINGS COME FROM GOD

> *1. background paper*
> *2. crayons, felt-tip pens, colored pencils*
> *3. construction paper*

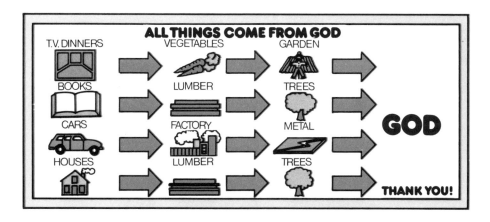

Depending on the size of your bulletin board, decide on four or five things that you can trace back to God through drawings. For example: TV dinners come from vegetables, from the garden, from God; books come from paper, from lumber, from trees, from God; cars come from a factory, from metal, from the earth, from God; houses come from lumber, from trees, from God. Draw each stage on a separate piece of construction paper and place across bulletin board with arrows between the stages.

At the bottom of the bulletin board put a large "THANK YOU!"

When the bulletin board is completed, discuss how all things begin with God.

Blessings in Disguise

Read Romans 8:28. Talk about how things which seem bad are really blessings if we trust in God. The cross was a horrible, painful way of dying; yet today it is a symbol of life. Also, St. Patrick was captured by pirates. He could have become bitter and full of hate. Instead he trusted in God and became a blessing to many (reread chapter 3).

Turkey Feather "Thank You"

> *1. poster board or large construction paper*
> *2. various colors of regular size construction paper*
> *3. tape*
> *4. pens or pencils*

Draw all of the turkey except the feathers on the poster board. Cut out. Tape onto a door or wall. Cut out feathers from the construction paper. On each feather write the words, "Father, I thank thee for _____ ."

On Thanksgiving Day pass feathers to each person present and have them fill in the blank. After a group prayer, each person stands, reads his "thank you feather," and tapes it onto the turkey. Repeat until all feathers are in place.

Share-a-prayer
Remember and list specific prayers that God has answered in the past. Thank Him for these answers. Share these with your group or family.

Tell Someone "Thank You"
Tell someone special to you—grandparent, friend, neighbor—that you are thankful for him/her because . . .

Indian Pudding

> *5 cups milk*   *½ cup molasses*
> *⅓ cup corn meal*   *1 teaspoon each salt and ginger*

This special dessert is similar to what the Pilgrims and Indians of New England ate. Enjoy it on Thanksgiving Day. Thank God for each ingredient.

In a saucepan scald 5 cups of milk. Bubbles will appear around the edge of the pan. This is the boiling point. Do not boil.

Sift into the milk ⅓ cup of corn meal.

Cook the mixture slowly for 20 minutes. Add ½ cup molasses, 1 teaspoon salt, 1 teaspoon ginger. Pour mixture into a buttered baking dish. Bake at 325 degrees for two hours.

16
CHRISTMAS

Trees sparkle with colored lights, people dash in and out of crowded stores, and children wait in line to talk to Santa. The excitement of Christmas is in the air. But there would be no Christmas if Jesus had not been born in Bethlehem about two thousand years ago.

Waiting is hard, especially at Christmas. Everyone is busy decorating the house with holly and tinsel, baking cookies and other goodies, and shopping for special gifts. But we must wait for the big day to open the brightly wrapped packages, and the suspense makes us tingle from our nose to our toes.

This time of waiting just before Christmas is called Advent, which means coming. This should be a quiet time in the middle of all the excitement to help us remember the real reason for Christmas. Advent also helps us understand what it was like for the Israelites as they waited for the promised Savior. They had waited for Him since God hinted to Adam and Eve that one day a Savior would come (Genesis 3:15). Families talked about this wonderful promise, and the good news passed from generation to generation.

Over the years, some of the Israelites got tired of waiting. Even though they knew the Savior would be born in Bethlehem (Micah 5:2) and that He would come from the house of David (Isaiah 11:10), they gave up hope. But others knew that the Savior would come when God was ready. All they could do was wait.

During Advent we tell the Christmas story once again. The miracle begins with Mary and Joseph. God sent angels to prepare them for their part in His plan—to bring a special baby into the world. Mary and Joseph had not forgotten God's promise of a Savior. They waited.

In a far-off land wise men studied the stars. One night they noticed a brilliant new star in the heavens, remembered the promise of a Savior, and followed it. They too had waited.

An old man named Simeon lived in Jerusalem. God had promised him that he would live to see the Savior. Time was running out. Still, Simeon waited.

The world waited . . .

Listen . . . A baby is crying! Hallelujah, hallelujah!

The heavens rejoice and the angels sing! The Saviour is born!

Mary wrapped her newborn baby in swaddling clothes and laid him in the manger. Soon shepherds came to the stable. "We heard the angels. They told us that the Savior was born today in Bethlehem. We have waited so long for this day."

Then the wise men arrived and knelt before the baby. "We have brought the new king gifts of gold, frankincense, and myrrh. At last our waiting is over."

After forty days, Joseph took Mary and the baby to the temple in Jerusalem. As they prepared to leave, an old man stopped them. It was Simeon. "Please let me hold the baby," he said. "I have waited so long to see Him." Then Simeon prayed aloud, "Lord, now I can die content! For I have seen Him as you promised . . . I have seen the Savior you have given to the world" (Luke 2:29–30).

Years later, when Christians decided to celebrate the birth of Jesus, no one knew the date. Some said that He had been born in a warm month since sheep were still in the field. Others believed that His birth had taken place in the winter and wanted to celebrate then.

Winter celebrations were common to the people. Two important Roman holidays took place in December. One was Saturnalia which honored Saturn, the Roman god of farming. It was a time of fun and merrymaking. The other was the birthday of Mithras, their sun-god. But these were pagan holidays, and some Christians felt it would be wrong to celebrate the birth of Jesus during this time.

However, in the year 354 Bishop Liberius of Rome ordered that the Mass of Christ (Christmas) be celebrated each year on December 25. It was a wise decision. As Christians honored Jesus during these pagan holidays, many unbelievers came to know Jesus and turned away from their old gods.

Christmas for the early Christians was probably a time to come together, worship, and retell the Christmas story. But down through the years, customs from around the world became part of this holy day.

There are many stories about how the Christmas tree came about. Many people believe the Christmas tree began as part of a church play in Germany in the fifteenth century. During Advent, Christians celebrated the Feast of Adam and Eve by acting out the story of the Garden of Eden. A fir tree decorated with apples represented the Garden of Eden. It also symbolized the coming Savior that God had promised to Adam and Eve. Gradually, people began bringing trees into their homes for Christmas. The whole family enjoyed decorating them with apples and small white wafers like those used for communion. Later, little pastries cut in the shape of stars, angels, hearts, flowers, and bells replaced the wafers.

In time, packages of all shapes and sizes appeared under the beautiful tree. Christmas gifts began with those the wise men gave to Jesus. Since Christmas is His birthday, gifts have a special place in the celebration. That is why we give to family, friends, and those in need. But like the little drummer boy in the famous Christmas story, our first gift to Jesus should be an unselfish heart.

From Italy came the familiar manger scene (creche) used in churches and homes. In 1223 St. Francis of Assisi wanted "to . . . see, as best I can, how He suffered the lack of all those things needed by an infant; how He was 'laid in a manger,' and how He rested on the straw, with the ox and ass standing by." So he built the first manger scene, and another custom began.

Christmas is also a time for music. The early Christians used hymns in their celebration, but it wasn't until the fifteenth century that carols (joyful songs) became part of this holiday. From that time on, people of all ages have sung these special songs in church or strolling along snow-filled sidewalks.

Another exciting custom is giving and receiving Christmas cards. It began in England in the 1840s and quickly spread around the world. What fun it is to rip open the envelopes, look at the pretty cards, and read the message inside.

In December we may also see the word "Xmas" instead of Christmas. When the Romans persecuted the early Christians, "X" (an abbreviation for Christ) became His secret name. Today in some churches "X" still stands for Christ which means Xmas is a special way to write Christmas.

On Christmas Eve our waiting is almost over. Boys and girls hand their stockings, leave a snack for Santa, and go to bed early hoping that he will come soon. Santa Claus began long ago with St. Nicholas. He was a bishop who lived in the fourth century in Asia Minor. (He was also a member of the Council of Nicea which set the date of Easter.) People knew him as a kind, generous man. There were many stories about his gifts to children and those in need. One told of a poor man's three daughters who couldn't marry because they had no dowry (the money or goods a bride brings to her husband at marriage). So St. Nicholas threw three bags of gold through their window and saved them from a lonely life. From that time on, people believed that all secret gifts came from St. Nicholas.

His fame spread to many countries. The Dutch called him Sinterklass, and the Germans named him Kriss Kringle. But in America he is called Santa Claus. He still wears the red and white colors of a bishop and is kind to children everywhere. We love him because he reminds us of the real meaning of giving—to give with no thought of getting something in return.

The waiting is over. Christmas is here! This is the biggest birthday party of the year. The gifts, carols, cards, and decorations all honor the little baby born in a stable long ago. The light His love sparked that day is brighter than all the candles on all the birthday cakes in the world.

> Happy birthday to you,
> Happy birthday to you,
> Happy birthday, Baby Jesus,
> Happy birthday to you!

> "Don't be afraid!" [the angel]
> said. "I bring you the most joyful news ever announced, and
> it is for everyone! The Savior
> ... has been born tonight in
> Bethlehem!"
> Luke 2:10–11

CHRISTMAS ACTIVITIES

Advent Wreath

> 1. *aluminum pie pan*
> 2. *four white candles*
> 3. *evergreens (plastic or real)*

Many people waited for Jesus' birth—Christmas. In the four weeks before Christmas you wait. Make an Advent wreath to help you wait. Cut four "X's" on the outer edge of the pie pan. Slip in four white candles. Place evergreens around outside edge to form a wreath. Light one candle each Sunday before Christmas Day and read: First (Micah 5:2, Isaiah 9:6, Luke 2:25–26), Second (Luke 1:26–38), Third (Luke 1:39–56, Matthew 1:20–24), Fourth (Luke 2:1–7). Christmas Day burn the four candles. Jesus—the Light of the World—came into pagan darkness (John 8:12).

"The World Waited" Skit

The following is a brief outline. You may elaborate or do less, according to your time and resources.
1. Adam and Eve receiving promise (Genesis 3:15).
2. Show promise being handed down from generation to generation.
3. Show some people giving up hope.
4. Mary and Joseph (Refer to Christmas story in Matthew 1:18–2:11 and Luke 2 for details.)
5. Wise men
6. Simeon (old man in the temple)
7. All people waiting for birth!
8. Act out birth and sing "Joy to the World! The Lord Is Come!"

Old-fashioned Christmas Tree

> 1. *artificial or real tree*
> 2. *apples*
> 3. *pastries (cookies) cut for ornaments*

Decorate your tree with small apples like the very first Christmas trees. Make wafer or pastry ornaments by rolling out dough and cutting into angels, wise men, camels, sheep, manger, etc. Bake. Hang wafers and apples onto the tree with string or red yarn.

Chrismon Tree Banner

1. *burlap 45.6 by 45.6 centimeters (18 by 18 inches)*
2. *green felt cut in shape of tree*
3. *white felt cut in small shapes*
4. *dowel (from hobby shop or lumber yard) or coat hanger*
5. *yarn*
6. *needle and thread*
7. *glue (optional)*

Fold top of burlap over 2.54 centimeters (1 inch) and sew. Slip dowel inside or sew onto coat hanger. Tie yarn on each end of dowel to hang banner. Make a tree-shaped pattern from newspaper. Fold in half from tip of tree to bottom.

Cut green felt into tree shape by folding felt in half and cutting double. Sew or glue onto burlap. Using the white felt, cut out chrismons (shapes to make you think of Christ). They can be any Christian symbols—star, manger, trinity, dove, fish, etc. Sew or glue these onto the tree. Cut out the letters "HOLY CHRISTMAS" and glue to the bottom of the banner. Use in your own home or give as a gift.

Birthday Party for Jesus

Use Christmas decorations for the party, making sure to have a nativity scene as a central piece. Bake a birthday cake and write "Happy Birthday, Jesus" on the top. Sing carols as well as "Happy Birthday" to Jesus.

Giving gifts is part of every birthday party. Have children decide on one gift for Jesus. We can give something from our heart—a promise to be kinder to our family, a promise to do a nice deed for someone each day, a promise to tell others that Christmas is really Jesus' birthday. Each person should go alone to the nativity scene and tell baby Jesus which special gift he is offering.

Bulletin Board—THE WAITING IS OVER

1. *background paper*
2. *pictures from magazines or drawings of children around the world*
3. *crayons, felt-tip pens, colored pencils*

Make a large headline at the top, THE WAITING IS OVER. Glue the pictures or drawings of the children in a large semicircle. In the middle of this draw and color a manger holding baby Jesus. Under the manger draw or place a construction paper birthday cake with "Happy Birthday, Jesus" written on it.

Make Your Own Christmas Cards

1. *white construction paper or typing paper*
2. *crayons, felt-tip pens, colored pencils*
3. *Christmas wrapping paper*
4. *Old Christmas cards*

Fold paper in half. Decorate the front with Christmas designs you draw, or cut from wrapping paper and from old Christmas cards. Inside write, "It's Jesus' birthday! Merry Christmas!" Sign your name and give to friends.

BIBLIOGRAPHY

Barnett, James H. *The American Christmas*. New York: The Macmillan Co., 1954.

Bartlett, Robert Merrill. *Thanksgiving Day*. New York: Thomas Y. Crowell Co., 1965.

Borten, Helen. *Halloween*. New York: Thomas Y. Crowell Co., 1965.

Bulla, Clyde Robert. *St. Valentine's Day*. New York: Thomas Y. Crowell Co., 1965.

Burnett, Bernice. *The First Book of Holidays*. New York: Franklin Watts, Inc., 1955.

Cantwell, Mary. *St. Patrick's Day*. New York: Thomas Y. Crowell Co., 1967.

Children's Stories of the Bible from the Old and New Testament. New York: G. R. Book Co., 1968.

Douglas, George William. *American Book of Days*. New York: H. W. Wilson Co., 1937.

Durant, Will. *The Story of Civilization, The Age of Faith*. Vol. 4. New York: Simon & Schuster, 1950. Pages 83–84.

Encyclopedia Americana. "Saint Patrick." Vol. 21. New York: Grolier, Inc., 1977. Pages 402–3.

Encyclopedia Britannica. "Saint Patrick." Vol. 13. Chicago: Encyclopedia Britannica, Inc., 1977. Pages 1076–77.

Farjeon, Eleanor. *Ten Saints*. New York: Henry Z. Walck, Inc., 1936.

Gallico, Paul. *The Steadfast Man*. New York: Doubleday and Co., Inc., 1958.

Graves, Charles P. *A Holiday Book, Fourth of July*. Champaign, Illinois: Garrard Publishing Co., 1963.

Halley, Henry H. *Halley's Bible Handbook*. Minneapolis, Minnesota: Printed by permission of Zondervan Publishing House for Grason Co., 1964.

Harvest of Holidays. New York: Thomas Y. Crowell Co., Collier's Junior Classics, The Crowell-Collier Publishing Co., 1962.

Henderson, Yorke; Miller, Lenore; Gaden, Eileen; and Freed, Arnold. *Parent's Magazine Christmas Holiday Book*. New York: Parent's Magazine Press, 1972.

Hole, Christina. *Easter and Its Customs*. New York: M. Barrows and Co., Inc., 1961.

Ickis, Marguerite. *The Book of Festival Holidays.* New York: Dodd, Mead, and Co., 1964.

Ickis, Marguerite. *The Book of Festivals and Holidays the World Over.* New York: Dodd, Mead, and Co., 1970.

Jacobs, J. Vernon. *60 Short Talks for Superintendents and Youth Leaders.* Cincinnati, Ohio: The Standard Publishing Foundation.

Kainen, Ruth Cole. *America's Christmas Heritage.* New York: Funk & Wagnalls, Co., 1969.

Krythe, Maymie R. *All About Christmas.* New York: Harper and Brothers, 1954.

Marnell, James. *Labor Day.* New York: Thomas Y. Crowell Co., 1966.

Meyers, Robert, Jr. *Festivals Europe.* New York: Ives Washburn, Inc., 1954.

Mt. Vernon, An Illustrated Handbook. Judd and Detwiler, Inc., 1974. Page 108.

Myers, Robert J. (with editors of Hallmark Cards). *Celebrations, The Complete Book of American Holidays.* Garden City, New York: Doubleday and Co., 1972.

Patterson, Lillie. *Halloween.* Champaign, Illinois: Gerrard Publishing Co., 1963.

Phelan, Mary Kay. *Mother's Day.* New York: Thomas Y. Crowell Co., 1965.

Phelan, Mary Kay. *The Fourth of July.* New York: Thomas Y. Crowell Co., 1966.

Sechrist, Elizabeth Hough. *Red Letter Days, A Book of Holiday Customs.* Philadelphia: Macrae Smith Co., 1940, 1965.

Stauderman, Albert P. "A Definite Date for Easter." *The Lutheran.* Vol. 16. No. 4. March 1, 1978. Page 34.

Wyndam, Lee. *A Holiday Book, Thanksgiving.* Champaign, Illinois: Gerrard Publishing Co., 1963.

RECOMMENDED CRAFT RESOURCE MATERIALS:

Evangelizing Today's Child. A Christian education journal. Child Evangelism Fellowship, Inc., P.O. Box 348, Warrenton, Missouri 63383.

Teachers' Swap Shop. A Monthly publication sent to anyone on a free will offering basis. Sacred Literature Ministries, Box 777, Taylors, South Carolina 29687.

ABOUT THE AUTHORS

Vicki Niggemeyer has a journalism background which she uses in editing a church newspaper. She is a Sunday School and Vacation Bible School teacher. She is also a member of the National Writer's Club. Besides writing, Vicki likes to read, sew and garden. She and her husband Charles have three children, and they reside at McGuire Air Force Base, New Jersey.

Judith Ritchie is a former elementary school teacher who also teaches Sunday School. A member of the National Writer's Club, she is a freelance writer whose articles have appeared in *Home Life, Charleston Magazine,* and others. Judy likes needlework, plants and books. Judy and her husband William have three children, and they reside at McGuire Air Force Base, New Jersey.

ABOUT THE ILLUSTRATOR

Toni Pepera studied at the Columbus School of Art and Design, Columbus, Ohio, and worked at Graphic House, an art studio. She and her husband Fred, who is also a freelance artist, live in Birmingham, Michigan.